Endorsements

Anna has written an awesome book that explains the importance of women managing their own flexible careers. In the 21st century, businesses are now becoming more inclusive places to work. The 9–5 culture is no longer a must for many businesses, the smart ones are realising it's less about measuring hours worked, with more of a focus on outputs produced. The book explores how working flexibly can be done without hindering a woman's career and disrupting her home life too much. Inside you will get great takeaways, including tools to help the flexible worker upcycle their skills especially when considering a leadership role. Just because a woman has chosen to work flexibly, it does not mean she is not leadership material. The change is on the horizon for v _____ _____ ny still think they are not able to _____ _____ se of family commitments. Inside

_____ _____ la

NED London Football Association

Can women have it all? This is the million dollar question. Anna's research based book addresses the issue in a practical, tangible but always research grounded way. Packed with tips and exercises, she challenges the notion that ambition needs to take a back seat to juggle work–life balance. This is an empowering approach, as we need to start with ourselves to challenge the corporate Always On culture.

Dr Almuth McDowall
Professor of Organisational Psychology,
Birkbeck University of London

Balancing career and family is hard. *#Upcycle Your Job* is a welcome and timely guide that reminds us that for women (and men, too) you **can** take control of your corporate life. This book shows you how. Blending unique and pragmatic tools with a solid evidence based approach that draws on the research and expertise of leading work–life thinkers, it provides a step guide to making sustainable change to achieve the right balance between work and career. My own research in the *Modern Families Index* tells us that all too often working mothers (and increasingly, fathers) are deliberately limiting their careers to find work–life balance. It doesn't have to be this way, and *#Upcycle Your Job* shows how to do it differently, and better.

Jonathan Swan
Head of Research, Policy and Communications,
Working Families

This book is a fantastic resource for working mothers who want to stay in the corporate world and find a better balance between work and family and for companies who want to benefit from agile working. It's packed with useful insights, fresh approaches and very practical advice. Women who are working smarter, job crafting and upcycling are pioneering a better experience of work for everyone and this book provides the route map to making it work.

Elizabeth Divver
Group HR Director, The Big Issue

Despite the overwhelming evidence that flexible and reduced hours support the progression of careers for working mothers, finding that flexibility remains tough in many organisations. This evidence based book will empower ambitious women to define and manage their own flexibility within the corporate environment to the benefit of both employer and employee.

Ben Wilson
Executive Director, EHRC

There is growing evidence that flexible/agile working and the need to be 'Always On' can threaten wellbeing and job performance. Written by an acknowledged expert in work–life balance, this rigorously researched but practical book helps you to find a better, more balanced way of working that also benefits your wellbeing, effectiveness and productivity. It considers the challenges that working mothers face when managing their job and career and introduces a new model that you can apply to your own life in order to take control and have a more balanced future.

Dr Gail Kinman
Professor of Occupational Health Psychology,
University of Bedfordshire

#UPCYCLE YOUR JOB

The smart way to balance family life & career

ANNA MELLER

First published in Great Britain by Practical Inspiration Publishing, 2019

ISBN 978-1-78860-074-3

 Practical Inspiration
PUBLISHING

Contents

Contents

Foreword

Career-life balance is a challenge that most of us – especially working mothers – struggle with throughout periods of our working lives regardless of the jobs we hold, our family backgrounds, or the country in which we reside. The effective management of work–life relationships matters not only for our careers, families, and personal satisfaction, but also for our productivity and wellbeing on and off the job.

Given the importance of managing career-life balance for women's health, their families, and societal gender equality, over my career I have conducted seminal work-family research and leadership development to help advance the work–life movement, toward more sustainable careers. Elected the first President of the Work Family Researchers Network, and a Fellow in two scientific academies: the Academy of Management and the American Psychological Association, I have had the good fortune to receive invitations to speak on work-family developments in more than a dozen countries around the globe. It was during one of these talks in the UK at the British Psychological Society's Work–Life Balance working group, where I first met Anna Meller about a decade ago. Starting in the late-2000s, I traveled to the UK every year or every other year to give invited talks on current developments in work and family and managing work–life boundaries, flexibility, and interventions. Anna and I would interact at these gatherings of professionals who were interested in learning about state-of-the-art work-family research and practice.

During these conversations, what impressed me about Anna was not only her passion for helping individuals and organizations to improve work–life practices, but her commitment to keeping up with the latest research on work and family and engaging in ongoing dialogue with work–life academics. Throughout my career, I have often witnessed a research to practice separation of the work–life communities; where academics tend to congregate with other academics, and practitioners and consultants with each other. Such a social division leads to a lack of conversation and learning across communities of practice on a growing societal challenge. The research to practice gap negatively impedes the transfer of best evidence-based research to the field; and also knowledge transfer in the other direction – where academics learn about the most challenging work–life problems facing individuals and companies and how to overcome barriers to implementation of best practice.

Individuals such as Anna are able to bridge this research-practice gap and promote learning and updated discovery across practical and scholarly fields. It is no surprise to me that Anna is the author of this book, *#Upcycle Your Job: The Smart Way to Balance Family Life and Career*, as she was able to draw on her knowledge-bridging background and many years of consulting in the UK.

Anna organizes the book into three sections. In Part 1, she summarizes why many of the current strategies women are following to manage work and family are not working. Anna shows an ability to strip down and focus on the essence of issues in an easy to understand manner. For example, she clearly identifies the three main 'choices' working mothers see for managing motherhood; and how none of them are working very well. These choices include: taking a career break but never being able to catch up in pay in lifetime earnings; working part-time but ending up working more hours than the pay cut; or working full-time but having careers stalled anyway as mothers try to control hours or demands.

In this section and throughout the book, Anna also shows an ability to integrate and provide a high-level overview of some of the current issues perpetuating many women's work-family challenges by integrating a number of current research-based concepts in a simplified streamlined explanation. For example, she discusses employer preferences for 'ideal workers' – those workers who act as if their job demands always come first over their families and personal lives; and 'the flexibility stigma' – the backlash that many workers (often women) face for working flexibly – terms that researcher Joan Williams helped popularize in research reports and books.

Anna also applies some current gender discrimination and organizational behavior concepts to the work–life conversation. An example is 'implicit bias' – the almost automatic assumptions that colleagues make about women who don't pretend to work 80-hour weeks, and how these perceptions can stall women's careers. Another example of the useful application of organizational behavior concepts to the work–life terrain involves 'job crafting'. Job crafting was coined by researchers Amy Wrzesniewski and Jane Dutton when they observed that employees often do it; and involves changing physical, relational, or cognitive boundaries of their jobs to add meaning to their lives. Readers will appreciate the simplified explanations of these relevant social science concepts.

Anna also refers to agency theory and notes that women do have more agency than socialized to believe. She then concludes this section with the presentation of the PROPEL model that women have the agency to apply to improve their working lives.

Part 2, Your Tailored #Upcycling Strategy, is the heart of the book. Organized into six chapters, it takes you on the content journey of many topics: work–life preferences, roles, options, possibilities, skills, and leadership. Readers will find many meaningful questions and tips that they can use to diagnose, reflect, and make a plan to improve their work–life situations. They will be able to experience work–life coaching and likely move forward on strategies for work–life improvement. I especially enjoyed the 'work out' questions in the possibilities chapter. Readers are asked to make a list of their job tasks and reflect on how to discard low-value tasks and focus more on those that are of the highest value. In Chapter 7, key skills for flexible working are identified. This is a great list of competencies for individuals and companies to develop and support. All of us over the course of the career, regardless of where we are in the child or elder care life stages, can benefit from work–life coaching and taking a step back to refocus on activities that best fit our calling and/or improving our flexibility skills in order to upcycle our lives.

Part 3 offers closing thoughts. We are encouraged to draw on principles of positive psychology to manage change. Such an approach moves dialogue away from focussing on barriers and why something can't be done, toward a conversation on solutions and possibilities.

In conclusion, career-life balance is something that many high-talent individuals care deeply about as they seek to excel not only in their careers but also in their personal lives. That is one reason I first wrote the book: *CEO of Me: Creating a Life That Works in the Flexible Job Age*, which focusses on the different ways in which we integrate, separate, or shift how we manage work–life boundaries in ways that align with our identities and give us greater control in our increasingly 24-7 connected world. Through my research, consulting, and personal life experiences, I learned that in our digital world, it is important to challenge ourselves to continually learn, reassess, and improve how well we are 'walking the work–life talk'. Based on her years of experience working with clients, Anna's book will help readers do exactly that – assess how to better navigate the ongoing career-life balance journey at pivotal times in their lives in order to close what Professor Jeff Pfeffer refers to as the 'knowing-doing gap' on work–life issues.

Dr. Ellen Ernst Kossek,
Basil S. Turner Professor of Management,
Purdue University,
West Lafayette, Indiana, USA, 2018

Introduction

Imagine a younger version of you. An ambitious recent graduate now working in the perfect first job at the start of her professional journey. You're excited, hopeful, committed to your career. You've just bought your first 'power suit' which cost an arm and a leg but was well worth it. It's a fabulous designer creation that makes you feel great when you wear it to those important meetings and interviews.

Fast forward ten years and the suit is still in your wardrobe, still looking great. You've taken good care of it, but you've not really thought about it recently as you've been undergoing some big life changes. Now you're ready to put it on again – and when you do it no longer seems to fit. Somehow it seems to restrict your movement and doesn't quite reflect who you are any more. You still like it and remember how great it used to make you feel. So what do you do? You have two choices – discard it or upcycle it.

Now imagine we're not talking about a suit, but about the corporate career you've been developing for the past ten years. Since you became a mother it – like the suit – no longer seems to fit. What are you going to do?

Every year thousands of women discard a corporate career that no longer seems to fit their lifestyle. It's a decision that could cost them up to £300,000 over their working lives; but it doesn't have to be like this. In an era where we upcycle other parts of our lives, why not upcycle your corporate career?

When I search for an online definition of upcycling I learn that it means to improve something we would otherwise discard in such a way that we create something of higher quality or value than the original.

There's been an exponential rise in the popularity of upcycling in recent years. When we upcycle we take an item of clothing or furniture we may have once loved – or where we see the potential for creating something we will love. Where we were once tempted to discard our belongings as they got older, now we're consciously choosing to transform them into something better.

When we upcycle we'll often draw on skills passed down to us by our mothers and grandmothers. Then we'll add a modern twist – perhaps an eco-conscious paint or an up to date restyle of a jacket. And voila! We're left with an item that reflects our new lifestyle. One that we can love all over again.

For some time I've been thinking about applying those same principles to our jobs and our careers. There's a lot about the corporate world that needs upcycling: cultures based on mid 20th century norms; working practices out of line with 21st century social expectations; models of career progression grounded in outdated stereotypes. We'll be considering all of these in detail in Part 1.

As a consequence, when we transition to parenthood too many of us discard the careers we've been working so hard to build. Sometimes we're seduced into thinking that something new will suit us better. We believe becoming a mumpreneur is our best choice.

And sometimes we simply feel we have no choice. Intransigent corporate cultures refuse to adjust to the new shape our lives have taken. We cut our cloth according to our circumstances. So we take a step back onto the 'mommy track' or decide to take a break until our offspring are ready for school.

These are costly decisions; and in many cases our earnings potential will never recover.

What if I told you there was a better way?

Women started breaching the corporate world in large numbers during the 1960s and 1970s as the economic boom fuelled demand for labour. They encountered workplaces set up for 'ideal workers' – organisations that ignored women's dual roles as both caregivers and employees. For over half a century we've been waiting for employers to shift culture and mind-set. And the lack of women in the top layers of the pyramid confirms that progress has been slow – we're still waiting.

Just as our mothers and grandmothers took things into their own hands, so it's time for new generations of women to do the same. As an organisational psychologist and work–life balance expert I know it's possible to restructure your working arrangement in ways that will both make you more productive and support your work–life balance.

The idea is to empower you – as an ambitious professional woman – to develop a personal route map that supports you in navigating both your work–life balance needs and your workplace culture. I want to open your eyes to new possibilities and inspire in you the confidence that you can be a Balanced Leader.

Why this book?

Recent years have seen a steady stream of books by high profile role models sharing their corporate journey. Women are hungry for new role models so that should be a good thing, right? While these books are inspirational the challenge lies in applying their wisdom to our own – often very different – life circumstances.

For the past 25 years I've been consulting on work–life balance matters in the corporate world. I've supported both private and public sector clients to improve work–life balance policies and practices. I've trained and coached women to make those small adjustments that make such a big impact when it comes to finding a balance that works for them. I've conducted ground breaking research into the work–life balance challenges faced by professional women. And as I've learnt more about the research evidence I've shared this with a wide range of audiences.

Based on all this, I've developed a practical six step process – PROPEL – that will enable you to create a working and living arrangement that meets your specific work–life balance needs while supporting you to remain on the corporate career ladder: so you get to lean in on your terms. The first two steps will help you pinpoint your own work–life balance Preferences and how you can combine the Roles of parent and employee in ways that support balance rather than creating conflict.

Steps three and four offer practical advice on how to upcycle your job for better balance. You'll consider the Options open to you – given the nature of your employer's corporate culture; and the Possibilities for restructuring your work. Step five provides an opportunity to evaluate your Essential skills. And finally, in step six I offer a new model of Balanced Leadership.

Think of it as three projects that will show you how to upcycle your work–life balance, your working practices and your leadership skills.

As with any upcycling project we'll strip out what's no longer working; reshape our pared down structure; and assess our current skills and resources. This will result in the clarity of focus we need to create a life that makes us smile.

What to expect from this book

The book is laid out in three parts. In the first I've provided a summary of the complex issues that get in the way of women's corporate career progression and what we can do to change the situation. I hope you'll find this background useful, but if you're itching to upcycle your own work–life balance you can jump straight into Part 2 (leaving Part 1 for bedtime reading at a later date).

Part 2 provides you with the opportunity to work through the PROPEL process, understand each step and apply it to your own life. The result is a more balanced life and a new way of thinking about Balanced Leadership.

Part 3 introduces two powerful techniques from the school of positive psychology that you will find useful in navigating a more balanced future. Again, you don't need to read Part 3 to gain the benefits of the PROPEL model. However, if you're unfamiliar with the techniques discussed (Appreciative Inquiry and Solutions Focus) you will benefit from understanding the new – and very different – approaches to change taken by them.

I've tried to keep the theory to a minimum. But I'm assuming that as a smart and ambitious professional woman you want to know why I'm suggesting a particular approach. And as a proponent of evidence based practice I want to demonstrate why the approach works.

So, before you discard your corporate career join me in the pages of this book. I want to inspire you to upcycle it instead – so you can be your best self and offer your best contribution to the world. You'll discover how much potential you have to upcycle your life. And the positive impact that will make on your wellbeing and your finances will delight you.

PART 1

PREPARING TO #UPCYCLE

CHAPTER 1

The three things we need to #Upcycle (or why women struggle to lean in)

Introduction

As I was writing this chapter the UK based Institute for Fiscal Studies (IFS) released a report revealing the wage gap in average hourly earnings between men and women had dropped to 20%. The gap has been closing gradually for all but graduate women.

The research also revealed the gap widens 'gradually but significantly' as women enter their late twenties and early thirties. At this point a woman's earnings are likely to plateau and the gap will continue to widen after she has children. The key factor in this according to the IFS is the impact that children have on her participation in the labour market. By the time her first child is 20 a working mother will – on average – have spent three years less in the labour market and ten years less in full-time paid work.

The evidence has been around for many years that having children impacts negatively on a mother's career and has costly implications for her lifetime earnings. In this first chapter I will be looking at the three persistent hurdles that get in the way of women's career progression in the corporate world: our difficulties with work–life balance, inflexible corporate cultures and the illusion of choice that holds women back.

There's no doubt women in today's Western economies are better educated than their mothers and grandmothers. They both attend university and enter the workforce in equal numbers with men. They're smart, ambitious and willing to put in the effort to achieve career success.

Fast forward ten years and the workplace around them begins to look very different. As they embrace motherhood they also begin to lose their foothold on the career ladder; and as they look along the ranks towards senior management men increasingly outnumber women.

In 2013 the UK Women's Business Council reported that women make up only 33% of managers, directors and senior officials. More recently the Chartered Management Institute noted that to have a 50:50 gender balance of management jobs by 2024 the UK needs an extra one and half million female managers over the period.

Meanwhile at board level in the UK numbers have risen to around 26% women for FTSE 100 and 22% women for FTSE 350 companies. (Globally the average is just below 15% female while in the US S&P 500 it's just under 20% and in Australia just over 23% for the ASX 200.)

Despite the fact that women have been entering the corporate world in large numbers since the 1960s and 1970s it seems the workplace revolution has stalled.

Why is this?

Is it because – as Sheryl Sandberg argued in her recent book *Lean In* – that women do too little to progress their corporate careers? Her advice was based on having a supportive spouse – a luxury not every woman has. Nevertheless, as we shall see in Chapter 4, it's possible to negotiate roles at home to support roles at work when both partners are willing.

Or is it because – as others have suggested – the constant bias and sexism women face creates a 'glass labyrinth' that's virtually impossible to navigate?

Years before Sandberg encouraged us all to 'lean in' women were already active in campaigning for workplace change. In Chapter 2 I will talk about how they made inroads into corporate practices that formed the beginnings of a roadmap for today's working women.

The interplay between corporate culture and women's lives is a complex one. The corporate world was built on the notion of the 'ideal worker' whose time and attention was focussed solely on his job. A job he would carry out day in day out until he retired. It's easy to underestimate the culture clash that occurs when we try to mesh women's more fluid life experiences into this model.

A further challenge is to recognise that both women's life experience and senior roles are complex; and that individual circumstances often require customised solutions. The purpose of this book is to introduce a new framework for this customisation – the PROPEL model – offering a new way for women to lean in on their terms. I'll provide an overview of the model in Chapter 2. But first: in order to navigate we need clarity about the things that get in our way and which we must upcycle.

Working mothers (and increasingly fathers) face three major hurdles.

1. We need a better way of tackling the problematic issue of 'work–life balance'. By going deeper with our understanding we can be more successful in finding what we're looking for.
2. We need a new strategy to navigate the career barriers that 'man made' corporate cultures create.
3. And we need to acknowledge the illusion of choice that pushes women into career limiting and costly decisions.

1. Our problems with 'work–life balance'

Is the search for work–life balance compromising your corporate career?

A wealth of both research and anecdotal evidence confirms that achieving a semblance of work–life balance is a top priority for women with caring responsibilities. Many are prepared to trade both income and career aspirations in their efforts to find it.

For example, a 2018 survey of London (UK) mothers by recruitment agency Feel Communications found half of those returning to work had changed jobs for family commitments; and that their degree qualification played no part in their current job. Six in ten respondents were willing to put flexibility ahead of a job that used their academic or professional experience.

The 2018 release of the Modern Families Index by the charity Working Families further revealed that almost one in five parents had stalled their careers and one in ten had refused a job or promotion in order to safeguard work–life balance.

In the previous year (2017) a Boston Consulting Group survey: 'Dispelling the myths of the gender "ambition gap"' reported 60% of both genders holding themselves back from promotion because of the perceived challenges of balancing increased job responsibilities with home ones. The report concluded that making flexible working more widely available would help overcome this.

A second Boston Consulting Group report from the same year ('Getting the most from your diversity dollars') acknowledged the provision of flexible working as a 'proven measure' for supporting women's careers. Other 'hidden gems' include targeted interventions around key moments of truth in women's careers such as return from maternity leave or promotion.

The Women's Business Council report mentioned earlier also identified the middle phase of women's working lives as the point when those with children experience a downward shift in career trajectory. This is often coupled with a downward shift in status brought about by unconscious bias – which we'll discuss later in this chapter – and a lack of flexible working options.

Thus, while countless research reports recognise flexible working arrangements will support women's progress, the reality is bleak. Research conducted by Timewise in 2016 revealed that demand for flexible jobs (47% across all salary levels) far outstripped supply at a mere 6.2% of all quality vacancies (defined as those paying at least £19,500 per annum).

Among women the most popular strategy for achieving flexibility is to opt for part-time hours. A quarter of the employed workforce works reduced hours and the vast majority are female. The pay and progression penalties they experience in doing so are also well documented as we saw in the IFS report mentioned earlier.

As an aside, both the Working Families and Boston Consulting Group research found little difference in the desire for work–life balance between women and men – a reflection of the changing social expectations held by younger fathers. This is both a cause for optimism and something we will revisit when we get to Chapter 4 which looks at how we can negotiate our roles at home to be mutually supportive.

Regardless of whether they have access to flexible working or not many women assume seniority equals a much heavier workload. Thus – as Sandberg observes in *Lean In* – women often hold themselves back from higher powered jobs as they anticipate increased demands on their time and family life.

Anecdotally this has also been my experience in working with high potential women. As we shall see in Chapter 6 when we work through the PROPEL model this need not be the case. It is possible to craft a flexible senior job – but it will require skill to succeed in the new working arrangement.

Are you clear on what work–life balance means to you; and what it is you're looking for?

Several years ago as part of a conference panel I took a question from the audience. Introducing himself as a coach the man in front of me asked:

'So what is the formula for a perfect work–life balance?'

I was unable to give him an answer – simply because no such formula exists.

Contrary to popular belief the solution to individual work–life balance is a complex matter. Thirty years of social science research reveals we have individual preferences for the way we choose to tackle it. Unfortunately there's a wealth of bloggers out there reducing the whole concept to a trivial formulaic solution. For example: women are regularly offered suggestions such as finding more 'me time' – the implication being that an hour in the gym or a relaxing massage will solve the problem. While both of these activities add to our wellbeing – essential for good work–life balance – they provide little clarity on how to develop an arrangement that feels comfortable for us.

Adding to the confusion the media has recently begun moving the goalposts – suggesting we should be aiming for work–life blend or work–life integration. As we shall see in Chapter 3, some of us will feel very comfortable with work–life integration but others will have a preference for separation. Encouraging a Separator to integrate or blend can be self-defeating.

A further complication is that when we combine preferences with individual circumstances we arrive at a variety of solutions. Consider, for example, the following coping strategies adopted by women I've met over the years:

Amy qualified at the same firm of accountants as her husband. After they married and had children she decided her best option was to return to work part-time. She realised – as we discussed earlier – this might potentially have a negative impact on her career. She might be given less challenging jobs and held back from promotion. But in order to feel in control of her work–life balance she was willing to make the compromise.

Beth was slow to qualify as a Chartered Surveyor after switching careers in her mid twenties. She decided to return to work full-time after the birth of her son so that she could meet her employer's expectations and keep her feet on the career ladder. Her parents offered to look after their grandchild. While the arrangement seemed to make sense, the reality was that her long working hours created friction at home both with her husband and with her parents.

Claire wanted to spend time with her young son and knew her employer wouldn't agree to reduced hours working in her managerial role. So she decided to take a 'career break' and focus on becoming a 'mumpreneur'.

Deborah was the higher earner in her marriage and had negotiated a working arrangement with her husband where he did much of the childcare support while she worked long hours. But as her daughter moved into her teenage years Deborah began to feel she was missing out on her children's lives and realised it wouldn't be long before they were off to university. She felt she'd paid a high price to keep her career on track.

Every one of these women ostensibly faced the same work–life balance challenge, yet solved it differently. Moreover, as their circumstances change over the course of their lives, so will their work–life balance needs.

The European Foundation for Living and Working Conditions (EUROFOUND) has identified three main phases of working life – each with different work–life balance challenges.

The 'entrance phase' is when we first join the labour market; and typically before we become parents. The challenge here is to establish a career and find a living space of our own. We are likely to defer starting a family while we do this.

The next phase – which it terms the 'rush hour of life' – is our main working and parenting phase. Challenges during this phase include managing conflicting work and family demands as we try to combine career progression with taking care of children and elderly relatives. We've joined the 'sandwich generation'.

While more and more women work outside the home, they still do the bulk of unpaid work in most households, regardless of the number of hours of paid work they do. Hence, for women in particular, the main working and parenting phase carries a double burden of work and family commitments.

Finally we enter the 'late phase' when parents are faced with 'empty nests'. We'll see later – when we look at the differences in men's and women's career patterns – that this can be a productive phase for women who find new energies for work as caring responsibilities diminish. Sadly, career policies in most workplaces neither understand nor are set up to accommodate this.

Achieving work–life balance through the various stages of our lives depends on a complex range of factors that include our own preferences for the way we play our multiple life roles (mother, carer, friend, employee), our family circumstances and the possibilities offered by our employers.

Trivialising what is a very real challenge for women by reducing it to 'ten top tips' in a blog is not helpful. We need to go deeper with our understanding of what work–life balance really means for us and to find clarity on what will work in our current circumstances. That's the promise of the PROPEL model.

Can you tell your employer you want work–life balance without being judged negatively?

Many organisations are inconsistent about work–life balance. On the one hand they acknowledge its importance for wellbeing; on the other they continue to operate with cultures that penalise those who openly seek it.

Ask to work flexibly and you're likely to be judged as less committed to your career. In addition you may be passed over for those challenging assignments that would develop that career – on the assumption that you want an easier life. More of this later when we look at how man-made cultures stand in the way of women's progression but for now let's simply acknowledge that in many organisations people are still forced to choose between balance and senior careers.

In a 2015 *Harvard Business Review* article Professor Erin Reid investigated 'Why some men pretend to work 80-hour weeks'. Looking at a global consulting strategy firm she found that women formally adapted to the situation where they were unable to work long hours in an Always On culture by reducing their work hours thereby revealing they were less than 'ideal workers'. As a consequence they became marginalised by their employer. Men – on the other hand – had evolved subtle under the radar strategies to 'pass' for ideal workers while maintaining a 50–60 hour predictable schedule. Shockingly when she revealed her findings she was met with negative comments such as asking how women could be taught to 'pass'. It seems she was disappointed that the organisation itself saw no reason to change its expectations.

Corporate cultures continue to uphold the myth that senior jobs must be worked full-time, require long hours and generally need to be office based. This is exacerbated by connected technology that perpetuates the Always On culture.

In recent years the corporate world has pushed work–life balance to the margins of the wellbeing agenda. Corporate solutions often mirror the trivialisation discussed earlier – with offerings such as on-site health activities, concierge services and limited access to emails during evenings and weekends. At the same time employers continue to 'help' staff cope with long hours by providing resilience training. For the most part employees are expected to take sole charge of their work–life balance. Very few organisations embed work–life balance thinking into mainstream policies and practices.

A further source of confusion is the conflation by many employers of work–life balance with flexible working. Flexibility does not necessarily lead to balance – particularly in the absence of structures that enable managers to craft working arrangements focussed on realistic outputs which can be delivered in manageable hours.

Given this context is it any surprise that women with caring responsibilities self-select into jobs where they know they can work part-time or at least without the constant pressure of long hours? As we shall see later in this chapter this choice is really no choice at all. And as we have already learnt women pay the penalty – in terms of both pay and progression – for this privilege.

2. The career barriers 'man made' corporate cultures create

Has your workplace culture been 'designed by men for men'?

In 2013 Maria Miller – then Minister for Women and Equalities – was reported as saying the challenge for most women is one of trying to operate in workplaces which had been designed by men for men.

Many of us are aware of the hidden prejudices women face at work. Indeed employers are currently busy training their people to be aware of this 'unconscious bias'. But it's not easily translated into the myriad of deeply embedded corporate practices that derail women's careers day by day.

The separation of work and home domains is a relatively recent phenomenon. It began with the Industrial Revolution – in the second half of the 18th century. The current workplace was established on the notion of an 'ideal worker' whose single minded focus was on his job, who was available for long hours and could travel at the drop of a hat. He had no outside interests or responsibilities, rarely got sick and prioritised work above all else. Most organisations still equate ambition with this absolute commitment to work – which plays against the structure of women's careers as we will explore shortly.

From the outset businesses operated with the support of what American economist Heather Boushey refers to as 'the silent partner' in the form of the Corporate Wife. Her job was to deal with anything and everything that might distract her husband from a 100% focus on his job. The majority of workplaces around the world are still set up to operate on this model: despite the fact that the majority of women now also work.

These outmoded corporate cultures are riddled with embedded and outdated practices that get in the way of women's progress.

Last year I spoke with a senior woman whose employer has a publicly stated policy of allowing all maternity returners to come back on reduced hours. As a new mother she had taken advantage of this.

When I asked *'how's it working out?'* her response was *'it's a challenge'*.

Why? Because she's the only senior manager who works reduced hours and who wants to get home to put her child to bed. Despite the reduced hours policy she's expected to attend off-site residential meetings where much of the networking takes place in the evening. There's no reason for this – it's simply the way it's always been done; and policy has not been followed through with changes in practice.

Of course she could press for change. She could – for example – suggest that meetings are limited to the daytime and that networking happens over lunch. But – as we will discuss later – it's not just the unconscious bias of other managers that's at play here.

As most organisations still operate on the basis of the 'ideal worker' the corporate culture will often punish a request for flexibility. Unconscious biases come into play and assumptions are made that the employee is less committed, less available and – having other priorities – less likely to put the effort into work. Professor Joan C. Williams at the University of California refers to this as the 'flexibility stigma'.

Most managers are given little or no training in how to restructure work or craft jobs based on outputs. For them a flexible working request is simply an inconvenience that raises doubts in their minds. Who will 'pick up the slack'? What will be the impact on clients, customers or other stakeholders? How does a manager who's convinced there is only limited capacity for flexible working within his team decide who is worthy or deserving and who should simply continue to work long hours? In this way flexible working becomes a 'concession' for 'deserving groups' – such as new mothers – breeding resentment among colleagues.

If you're a working mother then navigating your career within the context of these cultural assumptions becomes a minefield. As the website Pregnant Then Screwed so clearly documents many women experience pregnancy and maternity discrimination. And many are forced out of the workplace. Others – as we shall see later – feel it's their only choice.

Both research and anecdotal evidence confirms the unconscious biases to which pregnant women and new mothers are subject. And evidence of bad management practices abounds.

Male managers wanting to 'do the right thing' also struggle. Faced with an expectant or new mother many men assume her priorities have changed. She's bound to be more interested in her child than her work; is less likely to be committed to her career and is looking for a less stressful option. So they make choices on her behalf without ever discussing the situation with her.

Working mothers are all too aware of the negative stereotyping to which they are subject. Consequently they resist behaving in ways that confirm these stereotypes – psychologists call this 'stereotype threat'. Often they prefer to solve their work–life balance dilemmas on their own rather than be seen to act into the stereotype. Something we'll revisit in the final part of this chapter.

Can you squeeze your working life and career path into the male 'norm'?

Just as women's working patterns deviate from those of the 'ideal worker' so too do their career trajectories. The traditional corporate career model assumes progress in a full-time job with a fast trajectory in the early years slowing to stability and maintenance in the middle years and decline after the age of 40.

Researchers have amassed a wealth of evidence documenting the differences in women's careers but the corporate world is struggling to catch up.

First of all, caring responsibilities have a much greater impact on women's careers than on men's. Secondly, women are more likely to make career choices in the context of what else is going on in their lives – particularly their caring responsibilities. And finally, there's a distinct lack of women at senior levels to act as role models and lead the way.

Lisa A Mainiero and Sherry E Sullivan use the analogy of a kaleidoscope when talking about women's careers. Rather like a real kaleidoscope women shift the pattern throughout their lives by rotating different aspects of those lives.

During their early careers women – just like men – will tend to focus on career goals. In mid-career however (the 'rush hour of life' discussed previously) women are faced with challenges around balance; and family/relational demands now come to the fore. In later years women are often freed from these issues. They may still want balance but the kaleidoscope will once again shift.

Women are also more likely to change careers as they progress through life. Ida Sabelis and Elisabeth Schilling of Vrije University, Amsterdam refer to this as having 'frayed careers'. In contrast to traditional male career paths, research suggests women find a renewed sense of energy, purpose and vitality for work once their caring load has lightened. As we shall see shortly, organisations struggle to accommodate this.

What should we be fixing – women or corporate cultures?

Faced with the dilemma of women's stalled career progression most organisations began with attempts to 'fix the women'. Based on an assumption that women lacked the key (often 'masculine') skills needed to progress many introduced women's development programmes. These were designed to 'help' women understand the skills and behaviours they needed to progress.

Mentoring schemes have also become popular. A bewildering array is now available across the corporate world. You can find a more senior mentor, mentor upwards, sign up for formal or informal mentoring or perhaps find a sponsor who will both offer advice and be your advocate. Being mentored by a more senior woman is an attractive proposition for many but they are few and far between so they often experience significant demands on their time. In a further attempt to reduce the impacts of having children some employers also offer maternity coaches to support women back into the workplace.

While all these initiatives are positive and signal that employers are taking the issue of women's progression seriously there is also a downside. That's the risk of being seen to 'fix the women' so they can navigate the existing corporate culture. Since authenticity is known to be important to women this may not be effective for everyone – particularly if a woman feels she has to 'play a role' in order to make progress. What's more I've yet to come across an initiative that formally recognises work–life balance challenges and offers advice on how to negotiate a flexible role without compromising your career.

Many employers also provide women's and parents' networks. As we shall see in Chapter 2, when these were first introduced into the corporate world they were a powerful means for women to share experiences and lobby for change. Without a clear focus however they run the risk of simply becoming an internal vehicle for networking – useful in itself but not enough to change deeply embedded cultural norms.

The focus on women's development has undoubtedly provided opportunities for skills enhancement, but it has become clear in recent years this is not enough. The corporate world's response has been to shift the focus to 'fixing the organisation' and specifically to addressing the 'unconscious biases' that hold women back.

Some employers are now seeing this backfire. Firstly, despite the fact we all have them people don't like to be challenged on their biases and can become defensive. Secondly there's a risk that making people aware of biases can simply drive behaviours underground rather than change them. Employers continue to make commitments to calling out and changing the behaviours that inhibit women in so many ways. But putting this into practice remains a complex challenge.

More recently attention has again shifted to strategies that actively involve men in changing culture. Another positive step. But again we've already seen how young fathers also struggle with corporate cultures that restrict work–life balance. It won't be a quick fix.

In all these laudable efforts, there's a risk that we disempower women from taking action supported by a mature and adult corporate culture. The PROPEL model is designed specifically to empower women to take such action on their own behalf.

In Chapter 2 I will also be talking about the progressive model developed by the Families and Work Institute at the end of the last century and which recognises that successful change is the interplay of employer and employee and depends on moving work–life balance from the margins of the organisation to the mainstream.

3. The illusion of choice that pushes us into career limiting and costly decisions

How much choice do you really have?

Underpinning many of the barriers faced by women is the assumption of choice. While it's true the majority of women are not forced to have children that choice is made within a broader social and political context. In many economies that context is one which continues to reinforce the message that mothers have prime responsibility for childcare; and that women are generally also responsible for elder care.

Over the course of my working life I've come across women who 'chose' to work part-time in order to manage work–life challenges. Women who 'chose' to remain working full-time but move to 'mummy track' jobs where they felt they would be under less pressure; but also knew they would be less likely to be promoted. Women who 'chose' to negotiate a flexible working arrangement granted as a concession by their employer; and where they found themselves floundering to make it work in an inflexible corporate culture. I've also met women who 'chose' to take a career break; and women who 'chose' to refocus their career during maternity leave – often by starting their own business.

Two years ago I came across a book which made me question the notion of these 'choices'. It's a book in which Professor Barbara Hobson at Stockholm University analyses what she terms the 'Agency and Capabilities' gap in achieving work–life balance.

Agency is simply the term psychologists use to mean having a sense of control in your own life. Are you able to take action, make choices and assume responsibility for your own behaviour? The vast majority of us would answer with a resounding yes.

The Capability Approach on the other hand (developed by Indian economist Amartya Sen in the 1980s) considers what an individual is effectively able to do given the broader environmental and social context within which she is operating. What resources does she have that can be translated into Agency?

Having read this far into this chapter it should be apparent that when it comes to work–life balance a woman's freedom to make the most appropriate choice for herself and her circumstances is severely limited both by inflexible corporate cultures and persistent social expectations that she will adapt her life to take on the higher burden of care giving responsibilities.

We've already seen how corporate working practices, career structures and social expectations are built on the premise of the 'ideal worker' – a notion that not only hinders women but is also becoming less and less relevant for men. Enabling better work–life balance – for both genders – therefore requires a different interplay between employee and employer. One where the former is provided with better skills to improve her Agency and the latter adapts corporate culture to improve Capability.

Why is crafting flexible senior roles so hard?

In most workplaces flexible working has stalled at or just below junior manager level. As we've already seen there are many reasons for this: ongoing assumptions that managerial roles must be worked full-time; concerns about the impact on clients/customers; and worries about the impact on colleagues and subordinates.

Redesigning a senior role to allow greater flexibility is undeniably complex. But as we shall see in Chapter 6 it's not impossible. What often gets in the way is a lack of role models, a lack of knowledge around job crafting and a lack of clarity around the outputs expected – as opposed to the number of hours to be worked.

For many women opting for a reduced hours arrangement (unless it's a job-share) simply means trying to cram their existing workload into fewer hours while getting paid less and facing censure from the corporate culture. The good news is that we have mounting evidence senior roles can be worked flexibly – but it involves a learning curve and requires a systematic approach.

In many organisations positive steps are already being taken 'under the radar' but their invisibility means these are not part of the 'corporate learning'. Nor do they encourage culture change. For this we need a mature culture of greater openness and trust with structures that support job crafting and balanced working.

Did she go or was she pushed? Is leaving the corporate world an option of last resort?

In 2017 *The New York Times* ran an article with the title 'Inspired or frustrated women go to work for themselves' which documented the global phenomenon of women dropping out of the corporate world to start their own businesses. Of course there are many reasons for this – women may want to pursue an interest or feel frustrated at the persona they are required to adopt in order to succeed in male corporate cultures. Underpinning this choice in many cases is a desire for better balance. Not necessarily fewer hours since many of these women will work more hours; but the freedom to work them in a way that supports other aspects of life.

Similarly Dr Meraiah Foley at the University of New South Wales discovered in 2016 that Australian mothers were reluctantly pushed into self-employment as a result of childcare challenges and inflexible employers.

It's easy for women to be lulled into thinking being a 'mumpreneur' is the better career choice. A huge industry has sprung up supporting women choosing self-employment. Type the word 'mumpreneur' into any search engine to see the huge number of sales and business coaches offering women help with their enterprise.

Undoubtedly small businesses are essential to any economy and some will grow into much bigger businesses that bring new products and services to market. *The New York Times* article for example cites a number of high profile highly successful female role models including Sara Murray – the

UK founder of Confused.com. And some women continue to enjoy running small businesses.

But for others the reality is they will earn less while working longer hours than they would have done if they'd remained in their corporate career. They will also find themselves challenged to develop the same skills (and we'll be looking at skills in Chapter 7) needed to become a Balanced Leader in the corporate world. Sadly when they think of returning to that life the majority of employers and recruiters will devalue or ignore these achievements.

Whether they choose to be one of the diminishing number of 'full-time mums' or to dip their toe into mumpreneurship many women will reach a point where they experience a desire to return to the corporate world. This is confirmed by anecdotal evidence which suggests the number of women expressing interest in Returner programmes far outweighs the number of places available.

As we've already seen, women find themselves penalised on their return to the corporate world. Research carried out in 2016 by PwC with the 30% club and Women Returners revealed almost six in ten women taking a career break of several years were likely to enter lower skilled jobs when they returned to the workplace.

A small number of talented women have been fortunate enough to return to senior roles through Returner programmes and it's likely more will do so in the next few years. Carolanne Minashi from UBS while speaking at a seminar recently observed that these programmes open up a whole new talent pool for employers. It would be nice to think one of the consequences would be for employers to re-think the working practices that pushed these women out in the first place. Sadly Returner programmes often neglect to offer jobs on a flexible basis.

Most flexible working arrangements are negotiated with a current employer – often as a concession. Few senior jobs are advertised as vacancies open to flexible working. So coming back to work on a flexible basis is tough. The returner research mentioned earlier found 29,000 women returning to work were forced to work fewer hours than they wanted due to the lack of flexible working arrangements.

It seems the odds – and our choices – are stacked against us.

Where do we go from here?

In this chapter I have been talking about three big challenges to women's career progression in the corporate world:

- The problems and challenges arising from a lack of clarity around the work–life balance concept;
- Organisational cultures that create roadblocks, barriers and dead-ends for women;
- False assumptions of choice that push women into career-limiting decisions.

Against this backdrop it's easy to become disheartened, accept our limitations and buy into the belief that it will indeed take another 80–100 years before women achieve equality in the workplace.

However, if we shift our focus to possibility we become aware that more options are open to us. Tried and tested ways of working and of changing the corporate world pioneered by our mothers and grandmothers and supported by an ever growing body of research evidence.

It's these possibilities that will enable us to create a new route map for the journey to the boardroom. We have more knowledge than ever to empower ourselves and craft our own corporate futures as we shall see in Chapter 2.

CHAPTER 2

How to #Upcycle your corporate future

Introduction

In the previous chapter I talked about three big challenges working mothers face as they try to progress their corporate careers. In this chapter I will look at how we can overcome these and upcycle our jobs.

Specifically we will look at how to move:

From	To
Problems and challenges arising from a lack of clarity around the work–life balance concept.	Deeper self-knowledge about our work–life preferences and how to use this to thrive.
Butting up against corporate roadblocks, barriers and dead-ends.	Finding new ways of navigating outmoded corporate cultures.
Being lulled into false assumptions of choice.	Opening up real choice by pioneering new ways of working.

Our success will rely on taking personal responsibility and engaging in ongoing empowered dialogue with our employers. (Some might call that negotiation.) While it may not always be easy, it is possible. This chapter will introduce the evidence on which the PROPEL model is based; and which you can use to press your case.

Before we start I'd like for a moment to take you back 50 years. The corporate world was a very different place in the 1970s and it's easy to forget – until a film or television series remind us – how much progress women have already made. The cohort entering the workplace back then was mostly unprepared for the challenges posed by the 'man made' culture and found themselves bumping up against the notion of the 'ideal worker' at every turn. What's important to remember is that these pioneering women both adapted themselves to masculine norms and simultaneously pressed for change. They entered into discussion with their employers; and workplaces slowly began to adapt to women's more complex working lives.

Today we are in the midst of a new paradigm shift around how we combine work with other aspects of our lives in meaningful and productive ways. A paradigm shift occurs when our way of thinking about or doing something changes completely. The old rules no longer apply; the body of accumulated knowledge insists we shift the parameters of that thinking. The future success of your corporate career depends on you embracing that paradigm shift and upcycling both your work–life balance expertise and your working arrangement. To do that successfully it's likely you'll also need to upcycle your skills and your notions about what it means to be a leader.

1. #Upcycling your work–life balance skills

Harnessing 40 years of research

Contrary to any impression you may have gained from internet blogs, work–life balance is not a fuzzy concept best tackled simply by sharpening your time management skills and becoming better organised. Social scientists have been studying the subject for the past 40 years and some of the key concepts emerging from their research will prove invaluable in helping you get control of your balance.

Research into work-family (latterly work–life) balance issues began in the 1970s. It's a field that has been dominated by women – both as researchers and research subjects. Given a corporate context comprising 'man made' cultures and 'ideal workers' it was natural for early studies to explore the conflict between work and family roles. Conflict in this context can be defined as '*a form of inter-role conflict in which the role pressures from the work and family domains are mutually incompatible in some respect*'. We will dive deeper into this in Chapter 4 when we consider the various roles you play in your life and how they impact each other.

Early research focussed on both work-to-family conflict, i.e. how work interferes with family life; and on family-to-work conflict, i.e. how family life interferes with work. Psychologists consider these as two separate but interrelated concepts. So – for example – women would historically have experienced more work-to-family conflict as their caring responsibilities did not end when they entered the workplace. Men on the other hand were more likely to experience family-to-work conflict as they struggled to live up to the 'ideal worker' norm while feeling an emotional pull towards spending time with their children. Both can have a negative impact on wellbeing and job performance.

Conflict is more likely to emerge for those people that prefer to integrate their work and non-work lives. That's not everybody – research has also shown that some people prefer to separate the two domains. Separation and integration are discussed in more detail in the next chapter.

To add to the complexity the type of conflict you may experience will also be determined by the pull of the roles you play. That is, do you define yourself by your professional role or your parenting role? Which takes priority for you?

Feeling conflicted may be something with which you are familiar. It's often labelled 'working mother guilt'. It has an emotional impact which both saps energy and can lead to anxiety and job dissatisfaction.

The good news is that there is a way to reduce the conflict. In recent years researchers have turned their attention towards seeking to understand how our work and non-work roles can enrich each other. This in turn has led to the emergence of two further concepts: work-to-family enrichment, i.e. how does work enrich your family life; and family-to-work enrichment. We know that combining the two roles in positive ways leads to higher job satisfaction, higher family satisfaction and improved physical and mental health.

Chapter 4 will give you the opportunity to assess how well you're combining work and family; the extent to which these are in conflict and what adjustments you can make to improve things.

Finding balance with flexible working

One of the most popular tools for managing work–life balance is control over working hours. For many employers this has become the solution of choice. However, research has shown that flexible (increasingly rebranded agile) working is not a panacea. Fuelled by Right to Request legislation in the UK and driven by perceived productivity gains and cost reductions; it is often implemented with little supporting guidance on how to reap the benefits and avoid the pitfalls.

Research has identified a positive effect on health where flexible working arrangements increase a worker's control and choice. However not all flexible working is at the employee's request. For example, we saw in Chapter 1 that mothers are often pushed into part-time working where corporate cultures deny flexibility in senior roles. This is likely to have a negative impact on health.

Professor Clare Kelliher and Dr Deirdre Anderson reported mixed results when they looked at flexible working practices in the UK. They found that employees were experiencing work intensification (higher workload) as a result of adopting flexible working practices ostensibly promoted as corporate work–life initiatives. In my experience this is particularly likely where someone negotiates a reduced hours contract – often with little or no guidance on how the work can be restructured to fit into fewer hours.

Somewhat surprisingly Kelliher and Anderson found the employee response was not entirely negative. They suggest people were willing to accept the intensification as a quid pro quo for greater control and access to the flexible working arrangement. While on the face of it this may appear to be a reasonable compromise; it can in fact lead to the type of conflict we discussed in the previous section. In Chapter 6 I have provided tools that will enable you to upcycle your job in ways that avoid this situation.

A further challenge is the increasingly sophisticated Information and Communications Technology (ICT) that enables us to be available 24/7 and which is leading to what has been termed an Always On culture. In a survey carried out in 2017 Professor Gail Kinman and Dr Almuth McDowall found more than half of respondents said their employer had no work–life balance policy and no guidance on ICT use. Asked whose responsibility this should be over half of respondents felt it should be a dialogue between employer and employee. In the absence of that employer support you'll need to figure it out for yourself. And how you do that will – once again – depend on what you discover about your work–life balance preferences in the next chapter.

Taking control and living a balanced life

By now it should be apparent that managing your work–life balance goes beyond a cursory exercise including a 'balance wheel' or a simple list of self-management tips. Work–life balance is defined by personal preferences and likely to change as you experience the impact of both predictable and unpredictable life events. Finding the balance that suits you requires a deeper exploration of your values and your preferences. The PROPEL model provides a structure to support you in doing that.

Given its personal nature work–life balance can be hard to define. Nevertheless having clarity on what it is we are looking for is the first step to finding it. The most useful definition I've come across is by two Australian researchers Thomas Kalliath and Paula Brough. They suggest that balance is a personal feeling that our work and non-work activities are compatible and supporting our growth based on our current life priorities. I offer this as a guiding principle for working through the PROPEL model.

To maintain balance in your life it is essential that you regularly revisit where you are and whether current arrangements still serve you. Just as you might use new year resolutions to set health goals, so the start of the year is a good time to reflect on the structure of your work and non-work life; and whether adjustments are needed to bring the two back into balance.

As your career progresses and you move to new roles you will continue to face new challenges in how to structure your working time. The same is true of changes in family circumstances. For example, as the parent of a teen you may be surprised to find you want to change your working hours so that you can guide your child through key public exams. Empty nesters on the other hand may be keen to return to full-time work – unless the needs of an ageing relative begin to take priority.

A good work–life balance supports wellbeing and allows recovery time: both of which are essential for navigating the complexities of modern life. Maintaining clarity around what you need and taking personal responsibility to make it happen are the keys. This is true both at home and at work. Of course your employer has a role to play – specifically in developing appropriate policies and in working to improve the corporate culture – but the process of finding the right balance for you will only succeed as a dialogue.

Your efforts to upcycle your job and career are likely to challenge you to be a pioneer. You'll be demonstrating new behaviours and working to new arrangements. You'll have much in common with our mothers and grandmothers who did the same; and you can draw on their strength and wisdom. You'll become more visible – a potential role model showing others the way. And that will benefit not only you and your family but also future generations of workers.

2. #Upcycling work

Reaching for a balanced future

This is not intended to be a book about how to bring about culture change. But I've positioned the challenges of upcycling jobs in the context of existing and outmoded corporate cultures so we need to briefly discuss the topic of changing culture. First of all, let's be clear about what it is we're talking about.

The simplest definition of culture in popular use is: '*The way we do things around here.*'

When it comes to balanced working, 'the way we do things around here' is no longer fit for purpose. Academics talk about deeply embedded working practices that stand in the way of both women's careers and balanced working. If you want to upcycle work you will therefore inevitably need to upcycle your working practices. If enough other people choose to do the same that may eventually bring about a culture change – but it will be a much more gradual process than many of the radical change programmes that organisations implement.

As an aside, gradual can sometimes work more effectively than radical – as I saw in one of my earliest HR jobs. I worked for a financial services firm that introduced a new management training programme with a focus on embedding new behaviours. Over several years, as people went through the programme, we saw a big change in management behaviour. As somebody once said to me: '*change happens best when nobody notices*'.

Whether you are currently working flexibly and struggling with the load, or wanting to work flexibly and unsure about how to restructure your work, the focus of the PROPEL model is on enabling you to create a manageable job that works for your employer (and the people around you) while supporting your own work–life balance.

In that context consider the following:

- The content of jobs changes regularly in response to a range of factors such as shifts in employer focus; changes in customer demands and the introduction of new technologies. For this reason, when I was trained as an in-house recruiter I was told to always check a job description is still current before starting to fill a vacancy.
- It's for this reason that an organisation may also periodically choose to review the content of jobs across the

board. For example, when I worked at one of the GE Capital companies we were subject to their Work Out process. The aim of the exercise was to identify both redundant tasks and those that take up a lot of time for very little reward – with the intention of making work more efficient. I've since used some of the principles in my own consulting work; and have based some of the exercises in Chapter 6 on them.

- Researchers have found that job crafting – where individual jobholders make minor adjustments to their working practices to better suit their needs – is also pretty common. Indeed allowing employees to job craft has been shown to increase both productivity and engagement. Again we'll be considering the details in Chapter 6.
- The rise of Artificial Intelligence and how it will be applied in the workplace of the future is adding another dimension to the discussion about how we create and re-create jobs.

I'm confident you can upcycle your job. I've seen it happen with coaching clients. But a well-considered new structure will not of itself cut through an obstructive corporate culture. For that we need additional tools – and the ones I favour are drawn from positive psychology. In Chapter 9 I will introduce you to two specific approaches – Appreciative Inquiry and Solutions Focus. I use both in my work and I like them because (as the name suggests) they focus on the positive, on solutions rather than problems and on creating a better future. My clients don't get tied up in re-living the past and ruminating on what doesn't work.

The plan is that you use the tools and techniques in this book to upcycle your job while making the least impact on those around you. Of course your nearest and dearest – both at home and work – will see improvements. Should they choose to apply the same changes to their lives then the change will gradually ripple out. But to reiterate, we're not looking for big change initiatives. Our focus is simply on doing what's best for us and the people around us.

Corporate cultures – how mountains move

While I've been stressing that widespread culture change is not our primary objective, some understanding of how corporate cultures do change can be helpful.

There are many models of culture change, but only one that charts the journey of an organisation towards becoming an employer that truly supports work–life balance. It was developed by the Families and Work Institute (New York) in 1998 and published under the title: 'The Evolving Business Case for Work–Life Initiatives'. The model has five steps but for practical reasons I will only be discussing the first four. In my experience no employer has yet fully reached step four which involves redesigning work processes for better balance. (Although in fairness a few are getting there – organisations such as Unilever and PwC that are re-thinking their HR processes and working practices.)

The first step of the model focusses on childcare support driven by grass roots pressure from female employees. Until this point the guiding principle for the organisation had been the notion of the 'ideal worker' unencumbered by outside responsibilities. For many employers supporting childcare was their first recognition that something must change if they were to attract and retain working mothers.

In step two the focus broadens to supporting work–life balance for all families, not just those with young children. At this stage HR typically steps in to develop appropriate policies. In the UK (and the European Union) much of the impetus for family friendly policies has – in reality – been driven by employment legislation protecting pregnant women and new parents.

At step three the focus moves to organisational culture and to shifting it so that it supports work–life balance for everyone. As we saw in Chapter 1 many employers have yet to reach this point; and despite the widespread availability of flexible working policies many employees continue to struggle with their work–life balance. When step three is fully complete the hearts and minds of all employees have been won. The organisation is now ready for step four: to begin evaluating work processes. Jobs are redesigned for efficiency and to support work–life balance.

In 2001, on behalf of the charity Working Families, I conducted research into work–life balance in the City of London (UK). We identified a number of forward thinking employers on the brink of moving from step two to step three. Five years later the charity once again commissioned me to revisit those employers and identify the roadmap that will take organisations to step three.

I uncovered a five stage process leading from step two to step three. The most important aspect – and the most time consuming – involved focussing on changing conversations. Social scientists tell us that it is our day to day conversations and our stories which shape our lives and our organisational cultures. For example: James M Higgins and Craig McAllaster – writing in the *Journal of Change Management* – refer to these stories as 'cultural artefacts' (cultural artefacts also include role models). According to them we must change these cultural artefacts if we are to change the corporate culture. That means telling different stories about *'the way we do things around here'.* We do that by changing the conversation from why we cannot do something to exploring the possibilities for how we might make it happen. And we do it when we change the role models the organisation chooses to publicise. That's why sharing examples of people working successfully and in balanced ways at senior levels is so important.

Appreciative Inquiry – introduced in the previous section – is a change methodology based on conversation and storytelling. That's why I've included it as one of the tools that will support you. You can begin to change the conversations you have with the people around you. And you no longer need to wait for your employer to make the first move.

Upcycling working practices – then and now

Earlier in this chapter I pointed out that changes to jobs are happening all the time. It's easy to forget there was a time before job-share or term-time working were available – or even thought possible – in the corporate world. These developments were prompted by the efforts of our mothers and grandmothers who looked for working arrangements that would fit around their caring responsibilities.

The heavier burden of care continues to fall on women; and so we continue to press for changes to working practices. Since the turn of the century a growing group of pioneers has been demonstrating that flexible working in senior roles is possible. It's just over ten years since the charity Working Families published its ground breaking report 'Hours to Suit' documenting a range of flexible working arrangements at senior levels. More recently the social enterprise Timewise has been producing an annual list of 'Power Part Timers' – adding to the growing evidence that flexible working at senior levels is possible. Now, more than ever, we have the ammunition to counter the response that flexible senior roles are *not the way we do things around here*.

When our grandmothers wanted to find work they had little choice but to join the corporate world. They mostly acted out of a desire for independence and to generate an income. But many stayed because they learnt they could make an impact on the way we live our lives. It's the big corporates that determine what products we will find in our shops, what financial services we can access and how we spend our leisure time. The corporate world needs the contribution of women at all levels so that we can share our diverse experiences. But the corporate world has also been slow to accommodate us.

Working in your favour is the fact that the doors have been partly opened. Every employer has at least some policies and practices you can use to anchor your plans for progress and change. And the increasing spotlight on the lack of women in senior roles is likely to make employers more receptive to negotiation than ever before.

3. Putting it all together – introducing the PROPEL model

Why it works

So far I've been alluding to the PROPEL model – the six step process I've developed for use in my coaching practice. It's time to tell you more about it. The model is:

- Practice driven: exercises, case studies and insights are all drawn from over 20 years' experience of coaching, training and consulting in the private, public and not for profit sectors. I've supplemented my own experience with supporting evidence in the public domain.
- Evidence based: everything in Chapters 3–8 is grounded in academic and business research.
- Forward focussed: the model uses techniques from positive psychology that support you in generating new possibilities for the way you manage your work–life balance.

The model acknowledges individual difference in circumstances and preferences so it's not a prescriptive 'one size fits all', but empowers choice. As a consequence it can also be revisited when circumstances change. Rather than work out what to do by following role models whose life circumstances or aspirations do not match your own you will have clarity of what's best for you and the people around you. The end result is a personal route-map which generates stronger commitment from you to follow through.

It bypasses the need to wait for 'culture change' and equips you with the skills and resources to navigate your own career course. The focus is on fostering change gracefully by applying techniques from positive psychology. It supports authenticity and provides an opportunity to explore leadership – which will stand you in good stead as you progress in your career.

How it works

The model is built on the premise that confidence in managing your work–life balance is your key challenge. And that this is the concern which is resulting in you holding yourself back. Once you can see that work–life balance in a senior role is possible you are more likely to feel confident in negotiating and managing a flexible working arrangement.

The first two steps look at (P) your work–life balance Preferences and (R) how you can best combine your key life Roles to achieve enrichment rather than conflict.

It supports you in crafting a balanced working arrangement that both suits your needs and your employer's expectations. Step three (O) looks at the Options open to you against the background of your employer's current corporate culture, policies and working practices. Step four (P) then enables you to consider new Possibilities in the form of a job that meets expectations within that context. So you keep your feet on the career ladder while living a more balanced life.

Step five (E) encourages you to identify Essential skills and consider where these may need to be upcycled. It's likely you'll find the majority of these are the same management skills you're already using – it's simply the context that has changed.

The final step (L) positions your new working arrangement as an act of Leadership. Professor Herminia Ibarra (one of the academics whose work I discuss in Chapter 8) suggests that in order to grow into the leaders we wish to become we must first begin to act like leaders and respond to feedback around us. This step enables you to do just that.

For each of the first five steps I've structured the chapters so they begin by introducing the key theoretical concepts. A second section then provides examples of how I've applied or seen these applied in practice. And finally there's a list of questions for you to apply to your own circumstances. While my intention is to provide you with useful practical information I believe it's also important to demonstrate the evidence on which this is based. So you can understand why it works and be confident it can work for you.

The six steps have been designed to build on each other progressively. In the first instance I recommend reading Chapters 3–8 in order. When you revisit the steps as your life changes you can simply work through what you consider to be the relevant chapters.

Throughout the six steps you will find questions to consider. If you don't want to scribble in this book I suggest buying a journal in which you can collate your thoughts.

You'll find a summary of the PROPEL model on the next page.

#Upcycle your job in six steps
PROPEL summary

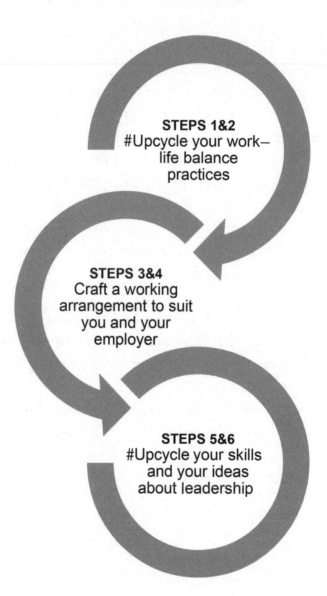

STEPS 1&2
#Upcycle your work–
life balance
practices

STEPS 3&4
Craft a working
arrangement to suit
you and your
employer

STEPS 5&6
#Upcycle your skills
and your ideas
about leadership

Clarity, commitment and courage

While I have been stressing that in many cases you will be pioneering new ways of working, I hope I've also convinced you that there's sufficient evidence to support your success.

That success will depend on clarity. You must be clear on what it is you're trying to achieve – both in restructuring your life for better balance and in creating a path for other women to follow. Clarity will support you when people and processes challenge you.

You will need commitment if you are to be successful. There are many ways to be derailed as the existing corporate culture clashes with your efforts. Most of the skills you will need to manage this will be the ones you've already been developing. Perhaps you can reframe your commitment in broader terms – as a commitment to improving the workplace not just for yourself but for your children and for the generations of women who will follow you.

And you will need courage. Asking for a balanced arrangement and managing it successfully is likely to make you visible. You may feel vulnerable and you may feel pushed outside of your comfort zone. Reframe this as an act of leadership which will serve you in good stead if you want to progress your career. Our ideas about leadership are changing: from command and control to consensus and co-operation – things that women are good at. See yourself as a role model for a better – more balanced – style of leadership.

Find yourself some support. If your employer offers coaching or mentoring discuss PROPEL with your coach or mentor. If that's not an option then can you find a mentor through a professional network?

Coaching with me is another option – but if it's just clarity you want feel free to email me. I also have a regular Balanced Leader blog where you can access more information. You'll find more details about how you can connect with me in Chapter 10 at the end of the book.

It's my wish (and my belief) that this is a book and model you'll want to revisit and reuse when faced with changes in your life. The model works as well for empty nester women ready for a fuller focus on their working life as it does for the new mother keen to stay off the 'mommy track'.

Ready? Let's get working on the #Upcycling…

PART 2

YOUR TAILORED #UPCYCLING STRATEGY

CHAPTER 3
Preferences

In this chapter we will be looking at individual preferences for managing the interplay between the work and non-work parts of our lives and how we can manage these in ways that support us.

Introduction

As we've already seen there was a time before women joined the corporate workforce in large numbers when the expectation was that work and home would be kept as two very separate domains. This was a considerable challenge for working mothers. Pretending their outside lives did not exist felt inauthentic to them; while on a practical level they needed changes to working practices to help them hold everything together. After all, you can't simply switch children or elderly relatives off when you walk through your employer's door.

In the intervening years work has come to intrude more and more on other parts of our lives. There are many reasons for this: from the large scale corporate downsizing exercises of the last century which intensified jobs to rapid developments in mobile technology this century which have intensified them further. Social and economic expectations have changed. More and more people struggle to find work–life balance.

Stepping into this scenario are the commentators who say that seeking work–life balance is outdated or inappropriate.

After all, they argue, work is a part of life so we should be aiming for work–life integration or work–life blend.

Research, however, has found that not everyone wants to integrate or blend. Some people prefer to separate work from other parts of their life. In this chapter we begin our journey by reviewing differences in individual preferences; and their implications for the way we live our lives. We will also consider the inexorable drive towards Always On working and how we can manage it.

Separators, Integrators and Vollyers

The theory

When it comes to managing the interface between work and the rest of our lives we have personal preferences. Some of us want to keep the two separate (unsurprisingly work–life balance researchers call these people Separators) while others prefer to integrate (i.e. they are Integrators). Rather than thinking of it as an either/or choice see it as two ends of a continuum. For example, you may be willing to integrate during the week but separate at weekends to spend time with the family. Or vice versa: you may want to separate but be willing to compromise and integrate on days off in case of workplace emergencies.

Separators prefer to segment work and personal life – psychologically and physically. When at work their focus is on work; and when at home they focus on the home. They prefer not to work at home or over the weekend – but should they need to they will carve out a specific time and space to do so.

As we've already seen separation was the workplace norm and the traditional 'masculine' way of working. In some corporate environments – for example, some professional services firms – this is still the case. Developments in mobile technology, however, have made separation increasingly more difficult for workers of both sexes.

Professor Ellen Ernst Kossek – a world class authority on work–life balance – further sub-divides Separators into two categories: work firsters (who, as you'd expect, prioritise their work) and family firsters. In my experience motherhood often causes women in this group to switch sub-categories. The emotional pull and social responsibilities of childcare will impact the priorities of a woman whose prime focus may have been on her career before her children were born. We touched upon this in Chapter 1 when we looked at how women's career priorities are likely to change through the life cycle.

Integrators – on the other hand – prefer to blend work and personal life both physically and psychologically. Historically integration was the strategy adopted by working mothers keen to demonstrate to employers that home life would not have a negative impact on their commitment to work. And so the myth of women being good at multitasking was born. We now know this is not true; and that multitasking takes energy as we switch focus between tasks. The downside of integration is that it may cause you to struggle with setting boundaries between work and family.

In her book *CEO of Me*, Professor Kossek proposes a third category: Vollyers. These are people who switch between Integrator and Separator strategies according to the needs of their job. For example: a mother working a term time contract may choose to integrate during the school terms and separate when holidays arrive. Conversely someone who travels long distance for work may be forced to separate during those periods while preferring to integrate at other times.

All three strategies have positive and negative aspects. So your personal preferences are less important than the fact that you've chosen the strategy voluntarily and it helps you feel in control.

In practice

Are you a Reactor? This is the term Professor Kossek uses to describe those Separators who feel they have no choice but to integrate. A combination of heavy workload and family demands may lead them to believe that in order to keep up integration is their only choice. Perhaps you feel pushed to integrate because you're working a reduced hours schedule and your manager expects you to be available to handle emergencies on your non-working days. Or it may simply be that you have been so busy meeting the expectations of others you've not taken the time to step back and consider your own preferences.

> Justine found that work was increasingly encroaching on her family life. So she designated Friday evenings 'Family Friday' with no technology, just chatting and watching a film. This is followed by 'Super Saturday' with board games in the evening and Strolling Sunday when the family heads out for a walk together. According to Justine *'Because there is a focus it strops drift…I'm now spending real quality time with [my children] and we all feel much better for it.'*

Conversely some integrators find themselves forced to separate – often as a result of the organisational culture within which they are working. Professor Kossek calls these people Captives – reflecting their feeling of being trapped in an unsatisfactory arrangement. They may be unable to access a flexible working arrangement or they may have a job that must be done in the office.

Over the years I've met a lot of mothers who are Captives – particularly those who are working in senior roles where the corporate culture demands long and inflexible hours. Sadly many workplaces still believe flexible working and senior management simply don't mix.

Finally Job Warriors are people who volley out of necessity rather than choice. For example, the parent whose job requires her to work away from home; and who may not see her children for considerable periods of time.

Working with your preferences and finding a boundary management style that suits you is an important factor in finding balance and maintaining wellbeing. We'll explore this further in the next section.

Spillover and boundary management

The theory

Regardless of whether we integrate, separate or volley the positive and negative effects of events and experiences in our work lives are likely to impact our home lives and vice-versa. Psychologists call this spillover (or crossover).

For example: positive spillover happens where satisfaction and stimulation at work lead to higher levels of energy and satisfaction for us at home. Negative spillover occurs when the problems and conflicts we experience at work drain and preoccupy us – with a negative impact on both our behaviour and our experiences with the family.

The thing is: spillover doesn't just affect us personally. It also affects the people with whom we live. Researchers have found associations between negative spillover and a lower quality of family life, greater marital conflict, poorer health and higher levels of psychological distress.

To date much of this research has focussed on the impact of a husband's job-stressors on his wife. That's because in the past researchers were evaluating couples where the man was the higher earner while his partner either did not work or had a more junior – possibly part-time – job. So very little is known about spillover in dual career couples. What we do know is that most couples are likely to discuss their work challenges at home. Talking to each other provides us with the support we need to mediate the effects of stress. But it can also have a potentially negative effect.

Professor of Health Psychology Gail Kinman and her colleagues have identified work demands as the aspect of a job most clearly related to the spillover of stress into home life for both men and women. For men, the challenges of maintaining personal standards and meeting the demands of others were the aspects most strongly identified as leading to the spillover of stress to their female partners. For women on the other hand workload demands and demands for quality were associated with anxiety and depression in their male partners.

One way to manage both personal work–life stress and that which spills over from our partner is by getting clearer on our boundaries. Indeed Professor Kossek (who we met earlier) believes one of the key challenges for many of us in the face of demands from our ever present mobile devices is how we disengage from a particular sphere – often that of work. We must actively manage our boundaries to do so.

Boundary management is a key area of work–life research. It can be defined as the mental processes or strategies people use to manage the boundaries between their various life roles. Put simply: a boundary management style is the general approach a person will use to demarcate boundaries between her work, family and any other life roles. Making a conscious decision to adopt a boundary style that suits us will help us feel more in control. And this in turn is likely to reduce the degree of work–life conflict we experience. We'll be exploring the notion of work–life conflict further in the next chapter.

Historically even those of us who preferred to integrate would experience a degree of enforced separation. This began to change with the advent of mobile phones and personal computers. The blurring of boundaries has been creeping up inexorably. Now the pervasive use of Information and Communications Technology (ICT) together with the increasing adoption of flexible working practices means most of us find ourselves living in an Always On culture. We'll look at that in more detail shortly.

Since Integrator and Separator strategies form two ends of a continuum we always have a choice to move ourselves to a different position along it. Some work–life researchers are encouraging us to consider the positive benefits of an active separation strategy against the backdrop of an increasing blurring of the boundaries in the new world of work.

In practice

Social support is an important factor in managing spillover. Research has found that women tend to find more sources of support among work colleagues, family and friends than do men. It's likely the crossover of stress from men to women is a result of men leaning heavily (perhaps exclusively) on their life partner for emotional support; and 'off-loading' stress – to the detriment of the female partner's wellbeing.

If you're one half of a dual career couple and your partner is in a stressful job you may need to reconsider the degree to which you can play the 'supportive wife'. How we choose to play our various life roles is something we will explore in the next chapter.

Developing a clear boundary management strategy that works for you has considerable benefits.

My client Laura was the higher earner in her marriage. Her job required long hours and a regular commute to London. During our coaching session we agreed a strategy that she felt would work for her.

Firstly, Laura told her boss that after 7:00 pm she would be unavailable to answer emails or texts until 9:00 am the following morning. She was surprised by her boss's positive response to this. Laura then spent her evening commute finishing up work tasks. When she arrived at her front door she would pause and take a few mindful minutes to switch into parent mode. At our next session Laura told me she felt more fully present in her family life and had discovered a new energy for work as a result.

Professor Kinman stresses that downtime is essential to replenish physical and mental energy and avoid burnout. She suggests several ways to set boundaries. One in particular is to identify 'corridors' to help you separate work from your personal life.

When you finish work (or return home) set a small amount of time to go for a run, do yoga, phone a friend (but don't talk about work), cook dinner. Sit down for a while and give your full attention to your partner or children. A small amount of time doing something different after work will help you switch off from work mode.

According to Professor Kinman the research shows we relax the most when we rest the systems we use at work. Her advice is that you see whatever you do to unwind not as wasted time but as essential to restoring your energy. For maximum benefit she advises being fully present in the unwinding activity and avoiding the temptation to multitask.

The Always On culture

The theory

The development of the mobile phone was initially a boon to working mothers. Now a woman could be at work and still supervise her teenage children's homework; or check up on how her child carer was coping when her toddler was unwell. Yet in just a couple of decades we've reached the point where this small device has come to dominate our lives and underpin our Always On lifestyles.

According to Ofcom 76% of UK adults had a smartphone at the beginning of 2017; while by 2014 our daily total media consumption had risen to 11 hours – an increase of just over two hours compared with 2010.

Dr Christine Grant – who studies the impact of ICT on work–life balance and wellbeing at Coventry University – has found that being Always On means our minds are never resting and we don't give our bodies time to recover so we're permanently stressed. And the more tired and stressed we become, the more mistakes we're likely to make.

Dr Grant's research has shown that people experience massive anxiety about relinquishing control. She talks about people burnt out due to travelling with technology all the time; regardless of the time zone they're in. And she points out that women are particularly susceptible to doing a full day in the office, coming home to make tea and look after the children, then putting in a late shift before going to bed – to the detriment of their own health.

In practice

Dr Grant suggests we need to become more self-aware of our technology related behaviour as a first step to managing our tendency to be Always On. Are we merging boundaries and staring at screens when we could be completing other activities? Developing self-management strategies is the key; and these are likely to differ from person to person depending on job role and personality.

Professor Anna Cox studies human-computer interaction and its impact on work–life balance. She recommends the use of microboundaries. These are strategies we can put in place to limit the negative effects of boundary cross-overs – such as receiving a work email at the weekend – so that we feel more in control. She suggests a range of actions such as separating work and personal emails/apps; consciously deciding when not to carry a smartphone; disabling notifications when socialising or turning on night mode at bedtime.

An interesting experiment conducted by Martin Pielot of Telefonica and Luz Rello of Carnegie Mellon University revealed that even a single day without notifications can be long enough for people to notice positive effects. While participants in the experiment were worried about being less responsive and more anxious about missing out they also found they were less distracted and more productive.

After the challenge the majority of participants said they would change the way they managed notifications. And surprisingly half had continued this two years later – suggesting that even a short break can be a powerful way of changing our habits.

If you're still sceptical about the need to manage your devices take a look at the TED talks by Arianna Huffington and Dan Gartenberg about the risks of getting too little sleep!

Applying this to your life

In this chapter we've been talking about individual preferences for how we manage the interplay between the work and non-work parts of our lives; the potentially damaging effects of 'spillover'; and how technology is pushing us to be Always On. Some questions for you to consider:

- What's your preference: Integrator, Separator or Vollyer?

- Are you currently working to your preferred style or are you what Professor Kossek calls a Reactor, Captive or Job Warrior?

- How can you make the most of your preferences – reducing the negative impact and increasing the positive?

- What do you think are the preferences of the key people around you? In the workplace? At home?

- What do you need to negotiate with them so that you can work together more effectively?

- If you're part of a dual career couple do you experience positive or negative spillover?

- Do you need a boundary management strategy?

- If so what would it ideally look like?

- Do you find yourself responding to the pressure to be Always On?

- If so, what strategy can you adopt to manage this?

- Thinking back over your working life: have your boundary management preferences changed?

- If so, how?

- Are they likely to change again in the future?

There are no right or wrong answers to these questions. The important thing is to identify your preferred ways of working and develop a strategy to implement them.

CHAPTER 4
Roles

In this chapter we will be looking at how we can combine the various roles we play in our lives to create wellbeing and balance while reducing stress.

Introduction

Have you ever stopped to think about where your idea of what makes a good parent came from? If you're in a couple relationship do you ever find yourself clashing with your partner who might have different expectations? And where did you learn to be a 'good employee'?

Social scientists often talk about the various roles we play and the scripts that drive them. A script is simply a series of behaviours we consider to be appropriate in specific circumstances. As we progress though life we will play a series of roles; and the scripts for these are often unconscious to us. They may be long held and are typically the result of social pressures.

For example, in a *Harvard Business Review* article from 2017 Associate Professor Ioana Lupu writes about the long-lasting and often subconscious impact our parents' behaviour has on our own approach to work–life balance. The participants in her research all said the same sex parent had the most influence on their own work–life balance choices. These typically went unquestioned until people reflected on perceived failures and regrets or were confronted with a traumatic event. At this point they made significant changes to their lives.

When we understand that our scripts are not set in stone, we don't need to wait for a traumatic event before we re-write them. We can then combine our roles in ways that reduce conflict between them so they enrich each other; and we find better balance in our lives.

Roles and scripts

The theory

When social scientists talk about Role Theory they are talking about the idea that our lives comprise a series of roles played out in accordance with pre-defined scripts or expectations.

For example, most of us have an idea of what the role of parent entails. We've learnt this over many years both from our own experience of being parented and the social expectations around us. We expect a parent to assume certain responsibilities for a child. Similarly an employee is expected to carry out certain tasks by virtue of having been employed to fill a specific position with a job description and a job title.

Since scripts tend to be unconscious, we're rarely aware of them unless they're openly challenged. For example, when two parents have different expectations based on their own scripts; or where adult siblings might clash over the care of a sick parent in response to differing social expectations. Similarly many women find workplace demands to be at odds with the way they feel they should be playing their parenting role – which often leads to feelings of maternal guilt.

A script often needs adjustments simply because the circumstances in which we're playing it have changed: as when children become teenagers or an older relative goes into a care home.

As we progress through life we take on, adjust and discard a series of roles. For example, we take on the role of student when we start school and adapt it when we continue on to higher education. We may then drop it when we start work or adapt it once more if we chose to study for professional qualifications.

Where did you learn your scripts? Do they still serve you?

For example: some commentators suggest women use the same scripts they learnt during their education when they go out to work. And that holds them back since the unwritten rules of work are very different.

When we're unaware of the scripts driving our behaviour we run the risk of playing our roles in irrelevant or outmoded ways.

Are you stuck in outdated scripts?

In practice

Once we understand we have a choice in how we play our roles we can make changes for the better.

A client of mine – the eldest child in her family – had always taken responsibility for supporting her widowed father who struggled with health issues. During our coaching sessions she began to understand the impact on her mental energy and how this was affecting the way she played her other roles of mother and employee. She chose to drop the role of prime support for her father and left it for her unmarried siblings to take over. They had to 'step up' while she was left with more energy to engage with her children.

We can also choose to adjust an outdated script.

Marie was the higher earner in her family and had the longer commute to work. Her husband acted as the primary carer for their two children. When I began coaching Marie she expressed the desire to get closer to her daughter who was just entering her teenage years; and was concerned that she'd missed her opportunity. The teenage years are often a time when the parent-child relationship begins to be re-written anyway. Once I'd reassured her that her daughter would benefit from more time with her mother Marie chose to focus on behaviours that would strengthen the mother-daughter bond; such as weekend shopping trips.

So how do we upcycle outdated scripts?

Our priority must be to understand any changes we make will impact on the people around us – both at home and at work. Small changes may go unnoticed but larger ones will inevitably require us to re-negotiate the relationship. And that may also impact the way the other party chooses to play their role.

Start small by trying out some new behaviours and assessing the results. Professor Herminia Ibarra (whose work we will consider in depth in Chapter 8) suggests taking a light hearted approach to change: trying on a new persona to see how it fits, how it suits us.

Making small adjustments to harmonise the various roles we're playing can be relatively easy. But there are times when we are called to make much bigger changes. Such as when we first become parents or when we get the job promotion we were chasing. To manage the role interplay at these pivotal points we need a framework that helps us take the longer view. That's what American psychologist Donald Super gave us.

Donald Super's Life Career Rainbow

The theory

Donald Super spent much of his life working on what he called a 'life-span, life-space approach to career development'. He identified nine universal roles we are likely to play as we progress through life (child, student, leisureite – a clunky attempt at naming the role of engaging in leisure activities – citizen, worker, spouse/partner, homemaker, parent and pensioner). Each role comes with its own script. Roles are played out in four main 'theatres': the home, the community, educational establishments and the workplace. Theatres act as cues for what is appropriate behaviour in the circumstances.

When Super developed his theory it was cut and dried that a specific role would be played out in just one theatre. Work would be conducted in the workplace, parenting at home and learning in an educational establishment. Over the years the goalposts have moved and now we find ourselves playing multiple roles in multiple theatres. Which can become disorientating. For example, the parent looking after toddlers at play who suddenly gets a phone call from an important client and needs to switch into 'professional' mode. Or the mother interrupted in the middle of a business meeting by a call from her child's school.

We saw in the previous chapter how Separators are likely to struggle with this sort of integration. Even for Integrators these sorts of scenarios create a disconnect between 'theatre cues' and role requirements. Navigating the complexities of working parenthood can be challenging.

The definition and expectations of roles generally changes with increasing age. For example, the role of child is different at ages 1, 9 and 17, and different again when the son or daughter is the 50-year-old child of an 80-year-old parent! At this last stage some role expectations can even be reversed, the child being expected to help take care of the parent. Similarly, the environment defining a role may change. For example, the worker role may change when someone changes jobs and encounters a different corporate culture.

The impact of a role on our lives is generally measured in terms of the amount of time and emotional involvement it requires. Thus:

The *temporal importance* of a role refers to the amount of time that playing the role requires. For example: students often fund their university studies through part-time work. However, that paid work rarely makes heavy demands on their time until they graduate and enter fully into the workplace.

Emotional involvement refers to the amount of emotion we invest in a role. For example, many new mothers experience a considerable emotional pull towards their offspring that can greatly outweigh the number of hours they put into their parenting role.

Super defined the simultaneous combination of life roles as a person's 'life-style'. The sequential combination structured the 'life space' and made up the 'life course'. Throughout our lives, roles are likely to wax and wane in terms of both how much time and how much emotional involvement they demand from us.

Sometimes, taking a longer term view and recognising that time or emotional demands which are currently heavy will get lighter at some point helps us make decisions which support balance instead of increasing conflict.

In practice

After three coaching sessions with me Emma felt more confident she could manage her work–life balance if she got the promotion she wanted. Her doubts this was possible had held her back for a number of years but now she was ready to move on. Except for the fact that her son was about to change schools and she recognised the emotional load on her would increase while she supported his integration into the new environment. So she chose to put off going for promotion for another year; and decided she would spend the intervening months researching job-share possibilities with her current employer.

Imagine a rainbow where each colour is vibrant in parts then fades into the background in others. And imagine that each of your life roles is one of those colours. Super called this the Life Career Rainbow. The waxing and waning of roles is represented by the intensity of the colour. Too many vibrant colours at one point is likely to represent too many demands on your time and emotions. If you've reached a point where all the colours are less vibrant you probably have scope to dial up the intensity of one or more roles.

What does your Life Career Rainbow look like?

Remember that how you choose to play each role is ultimately down to you. It's also down to you to manage the entire 'rainbow' of demands represented by the combination of roles.

A number of years ago I was part of a project to help the staff of a small not-for-profit organisation manage the stresses of their jobs more effectively. Several of the women were combining full-time work with parenting, studying for further qualifications and regular (almost daily) visits to the gym. While they saw this last activity as a way of protecting their wellbeing, I had to point out the considerable temporal and emotional demands they were placing on themselves. Stepping back and dialling down at least one of their rainbow colours was needed.

Role conflict and role enrichment

The theory

As we've already seen playing a number of roles in combination can lead to conflict. In Chapter 2 I briefly recounted how early work–life balance researchers tended to focus on this conflict which can take one of three forms:

It can be time based – where the time demands of one role preclude spending time in another. For example: a parent may want to attend their child's first nativity play or sports day. But an inflexible work schedule makes it impossible to attend the event and make up their hours at another time.

It can be behaviour based – where the way a person is expected to behave in one role is incompatible with behavioural expectations in the other. This was a particular challenge for pioneering mothers in managerial roles who were expected to act as if they had no caring responsibilities at home (once again, acting as the 'ideal worker').

Or it can be strain based – where stress arising from one role affects performance in another role; although there may be no time conflict. For example: the lone parent that has little support with childcare at home and always feels stressed when she arrives at work in the morning; or the woman who takes her workplace worries home with her. Again, in these scenarios Integrators are more likely to struggle than Separators.

Research has shown work-to-family conflict leads to lower job and career satisfaction, lower salary, lower self-rated and manager-rated work performance and higher turnover intentions. Family-to-work conflict results in lower life satisfaction, more emotional exhaustion and in physical symptoms of stress and depression.

In recent years psychologists have turned their attention to studying how playing multiple roles can enrich our lives – by acting as a 'psychological buffer'. So, for example, when we're doing well at work we may feel more relaxed about what we consider to be our 'parenting mistakes'. In the same way loving support from our family can help us navigate workplace challenges when things get tough.

When we see our home and work lives as being in conflict we're likely to experience a negative drain on our energy. We think: '*I've got too much to do in too many roles and it's exhausting*.' When we see the roles as enriching the totality of our lives we're more likely to feel our energy is abundant and plentiful.

How we think about the multiple demands on our lives is important. So how are you thinking about yours?

Spillover – which we considered in the previous chapter – can also be the result of role conflict. It occurs when we find it difficult to meet the expectations around two roles we're currently playing. As when our expectation of what it takes to be a good employee (work focus first) clashes with our expectation of what it means to be a good parent.

In practice

The majority of parents are likely to say that combining multiple roles leads to a more enriching life. While there will be times when roles come into conflict; the secret is to actively manage the interplay between them and make small adjustments to redress the balance.

For example, some time ago I worked with a group of local authority social workers who were required to be in the office by 9:00 am. This put them in conflict with their parenting role since they could not safely drop their children at school early enough to get to work on time. After a group coaching session with me they were able to negotiate a small adjustment to their hours. Simply coming into the office 15 minutes later made all the difference.

Professor Stew Friedman teaches Total Leadership at the University of Pennsylvania (we will be considering his work in more detail in Chapter 8). He talks about the four domains of life: work, home, community and self and suggests we aim for 'four way wins'. To achieve excellent performance in all four domains Professor Friedman recommends getting clear on what you want from and can contribute in each one. Experiment with small changes and manage your boundaries intelligently. That may mean identifying ways of creating separation between your various roles as a means of finding time for recovery. You may also find it's possible to bring two roles together – for example, taking your child to a company sponsored charity event.

The 21st century's rapidly changing social expectations provide us with opportunities to upcycle how we play our various life roles. We can re-write our scripts to facilitate better balance and make the necessary adjustments so we live with less guilt and more joy.

Applying this to your life

In this chapter we've looked at how the various roles we play come with expectations that social scientists call 'scripts'. We've seen how adjusting those scripts can enable us to combine our roles in ways that will enrich our lives rather than creating stress. Some questions for you to consider:

- What are the key roles you currently play in your life?

- Where (and when) did you learn the scripts for these roles?

- Have the scripts changed over time?

- Who is judging how successfully you play these roles?

- Are the scripts still current or do they need to be updated?

- Are you playing any roles which you feel currently take too much of your time or emotional energy?

- What changes do you need to make to bring these back into balance?

- Who do you need to interact with in your roles? What do you need to negotiate with these people if you choose to alter your role?

- What's your current experience of managing your work and home lives? Do you feel they're at odds with each other?

- Are there ways in which the two roles complement each other?

- What steps can you take to reduce the conflict so the two roles complement each other better?

- What other adjustments can you make to your roles so they support your work–life balance?

CHAPTER 5

Options

In this chapter we will consider how your employer's corporate culture, policies and practices are likely to determine the flexible working options you might realistically be able to negotiate.

Introduction

Research has shown that employees working a flexible arrangement of their choosing (i.e. not one imposed on them by their employer) are more likely to find work–life balance. In this chapter and the following one you will be preparing to negotiate that flexible arrangement for yourself. This chapter considers your current employer's corporate culture; and explores what's possible in that context. In the next chapter you will narrow your focus and look specifically at how you can upcycle your job.

The plan is for you to identify flexible working arrangements that are realistically possible for you; and which are also likely to resonate with your employer.

Before we start let me introduce the First Law of Cybernetics which states that: '*The unit within the system with the most behavioural responses available to it controls the system.*'

Since I first heard this several years ago it's become something of a mantra for me. It reminds me that the more flexible I can be and the more background information I have, the more successful I'm likely to be in any situation. It's particularly useful in negotiations.

As the saying goes *there's more than one way to skin a cat* (apologies to the animal lovers reading this book). Similarly in many instances there's likely to be more than one flexible working arrangement that will meet your needs. Over the next two chapters I will guide you to identify those alternatives as you prepare to negotiate with your manager.

Strategy: leveraging the culture

The theory

In Chapter 1 we identified outmoded corporate cultures as one of the biggest barriers to women's career progression. In Chapter 2 we defined what we mean by culture and learnt that out of the hundreds (possibly thousands) of culture change models in existence I've only come across one that focusses on moving an organisation towards becoming a better work–life balance employer. As long as women continue to shoulder a heavier caring load that's going to be a problem for us.

In her book *Women's Work, Men's Cultures* Sarah Rutherford writes about how mainstream literature on organisational culture ignores issues of gender. Those issues that concern women at work have been considered less important. And issues such as work–life balance – for example – are therefore approached as a discrete area outside of the culture that can be addressed on its own.

Dr Rutherford's book is an exploration of what she calls 'gendered cultures and behavioural styles'. The book was written in 2011; and I'm only just beginning to hear the corporate world use terms such as 'gender bilingual' and to talk about the need to have 'gender balanced' organisations. While this is encouraging it doesn't in itself mean employers have got any further than acknowledging their existing culture may not be 'female friendly'. Once again we're faced with the same choice we talked about earlier. Wait for our employer to change (and we may be drawing our pension before that happens) or take responsibility for making our own changes.

We saw earlier that culture is *the way things are done around here* and that it comprises a range of 'cultural artefacts'. Dr Rutherford's definition of what these are is more comprehensive than the one offered by Professors Higgins and McAllaster in Chapter 2. She includes factors such as management style, language and communication along with beliefs about work and how it should be structured.

Here we begin to see the first 'chinks in the cultural armour' we can leverage to our advantage. While many of the items on Dr Rutherford's list have been slow to change, there have been developments in the areas of management style and the structuring of work (aka flexible working). The catch is that in many organisations these changes are piecemeal and usually dependent on individual managers. On the plus side it does give us something to work with.

When a corporate client asks for my support with extending the reach and uptake of flexible working my first step is often a manager survey. Specifically I want to know both what flexible working arrangements they are currently managing and what other experience they have of flexible working – perhaps in previous roles or with previous employers. The amount of 'corporate expertise' that emerges is often surprising. And it's these managers that are most likely to be our allies in helping shift the culture.

I've discovered the best approach to upcycling culture is a combination of developing a very clear business case for the change; and harnessing the power of positive psychology to vision a better future. In particular an Appreciative Inquiry approach is very effective since it's a powerful way of identifying the 'hidden' organisational resources that encourage people to imagine and create better futures. Appreciative Inquiry harnesses the power of appreciation, inquiry, story, imagination, positive emotion and group dynamics. You'll find an overview in Chapter 9; but I wanted to mention it here because of its power in getting people to change their thinking.

In practice

The vast majority of decisions in the corporate world are grounded in 'the business case', so when it comes to asking for flexible working we need to develop a sound proposition. Coverage of the business case for flexible working can be found everywhere: in government documents, research reports and media articles. It provides our organisation with the intellectual buy-in.

Think of the business case at three levels:

The first is the personal. What's in it for your manager (and perhaps your team)? The obvious answer here is the resources he or she will lose if your health suffers and you begin to underperform. Taking it one step further: should you feel you simply cannot continue in your current arrangement and resign there will also be a financial loss to your employer. Typically this will be the cost of recruiting your replacement and getting her up to speed.

The second level is the wider organisational business case represented by the ways in which your employer benefits from supporting women to progress into senior management.

Finally, there's the external (PR) level. I've discovered that most employers value the kudos associated with an external award (such as Best Employer for Women or Best Employer for Working Families). At the external level there is also an increasing realisation that the internal setup should mirror the marketplace in which your employer operates. So, for example, lawyers have told me they would not be received well if they sent a team to a potential client and the team was comprised solely of white men.

Get clear on the business case for why your employer should agree to your flexible working request. It will make you more confident of your value which in turn will be reflected in your approach to negotiating.

But you also need to understand that a business case on its own will not necessarily sway your manager. This is where emotion often creeps in. There's a lot of unconscious bias around towards people who ask for flexible working. When you ask, some managers will still believe it's because you're less committed to your career; or that you're looking for a 'soft option' and won't pull your weight. Your manager may also have concerns about a resulting increase in his or her own workload. Or even that too much flexible working will create utter chaos.

You may need to have several conversations with your manager. It's these conversations that gradually win hearts; and eventually bring about change. Don't be disheartened if you get a less than positive initial reaction. Keep the conversation going. As I once heard negotiation expert Natalie Reynolds say: *'If a door closes then open it again. It's a door – that's how they're meant to work.'*

Remember to keep the conversation positive and future focussed. Do your best to rise above the negative comments and mindless teasing that reinforces the existing culture. Cali Ressler and Jody Thompson – developers of the Results Only Work Environment (ROWE) – call this 'sludge' meaning all those negative comments that reinforce existing ideas about how work should be done. In their book *Why Work Sucks and How to Fix It* they stress the need to eradicate sludge from the corporate culture. And while getting rid of it can be difficult, doing so will certainly move the goalposts.

Operational: start where you are

The theory

As I was writing this chapter I learnt that Mercer Consulting has a publicly stated policy of 'all roles can flex'. Several years ago I heard from its UK Head of HR that Unilever had taken a similar approach. If you work for one of these employers you're in a great place to have a discussion around flexible working.

That's not to say it will be plain sailing. Policies need to be put into practice and there's often a time lag while organisational learning catches up. What you do have, however, is a context where your employer is willing to work out the details with you.

For most of us, however, our employers will be slightly behind the curve; and some may even be downright resistant to flexible working. In that case you'll still need to work with what you have. As we've seen, corporate cultures are slow to shift, so our strategy is to meet them where they are and gently nudge them along. We do that because – to adapt the old adage – 'familiarity breeds comfort'. So we look at what's already enshrined in HR policies and available in practice.

HR policies – particularly around flexible working – vary both in scope and detail. If for example job-sharing or term-time working is specifically mentioned in your workplace policy that's a good place to start. While a manager may appear reluctant it's harder to be reluctant about something that's already in the policy – albeit perhaps aimed at more junior roles.

The culture in many organisations will lead managers to suggest the payoff for flexible working has to be a more junior position. Let's be clear: that's not what I'm advocating. Never ever compromise your seniority as a trade-off – that's not upcycling! (And as an aside, if you're contemplating a demotion because you're concerned about the heavy workload in your current or new role, wait until you read the next chapter which shows you how to upcycle your workload.)

In addition to policies, two other things you should consider are:

Firstly, what sort of flexibility is most likely to work with the corporate culture and what is most likely to prove difficult? For example, if your employer has a 'crisis' or 'firefighting' mentality this may get in the way of reduced hours working. On the other hand, if your employer is promoting 'agile working' that will fit nicely with your desires to work from home.

Secondly, what is your employer saying publicly about supporting women? Check the Diversity Statement and the Pay Gap Report if relevant. Public commitments of this sort provide a valuable context within which to develop your strategy.

In practice

When we start with what our employer's policies already allow we're asking for a small change that's less likely to be resisted.

Some years ago I was asked to research the pressures on senior managers in a London Local Authority; and to suggest ways to reduce these. A significant finding was that home or remote working – which would help – was not available to this group even though it was part of the flexible working policy. Since the organisation already had experience of home working and the infrastructure to support it, recommending that it should be extended to senior managers was a logical step.

Agile working too is on the rise. It's a strategy that's often driven by real estate costs while HR plays catch up. If your employer is promoting agile working then again you have a context within which to craft your flexible arrangement. Do keep in mind however, that with agile working there's a risk we simply work more rather than better as we're left to determine our own schedules. Ask for clarity on the outputs expected of you over a given period of time; and use these to craft a suitable working arrangement. This is particularly important if you want to work reduced hours. We'll be looking at job crafting as part of the next chapter on Possibilities.

What's possible will also depend on the nature of your role and the people around you. For example: you may be a manager who wants to work less than full-time. If yours is a well-established and experienced team then a four day week can work. Indeed, allowing your team to make decisions in your absence will provide them with development opportunities. However, if the team is young and inexperienced a job-share which offers cover over five days may be more appropriate.

If your employer has won an award for being female or family friendly – and it's worth checking as there are now so many awards out there – this can also work to your advantage. Occasionally I'll come across a woman from one of these award winning organisations who will tell me the rhetoric doesn't match reality. Calling your employer out on these inconsistencies can give you an advantage in negotiation.

Go deeper: tuning your radar

The theory

Over the past 20 years I've come to understand that when it comes to flexible working there's always more going on 'under the radar'. If you work for a big organisation you may be unaware of the working arrangements people have in other departments or locations. Indeed, in my experience even HR departments often don't know everything that's going on. Unless a flexible working request is made under the legislation they may not always be involved. Many decisions are left to managerial discretion. And while this does lead to inconsistencies and resentment, it also leads to hidden pockets of flexible working in various areas of the organisation. That Wednesday afternoon off-site meeting, for example, may be a flexible arrangement only close colleagues know about.

One of the reasons for so much hidden activity is that people fear going public. A manager will often say *'don't tell anyone or they'll all want to do it'*; while the employee with a flexible schedule may not want to be seen to be receiving favourable treatment. As a consequence working practices can often vary from the prevailing culture.

Now you know that it's likely more possibilities exist, it's a case of 'tuning your radar' to find them.

In practice

You don't need to be an external consultant to start uncovering these 'hidden organisational resources'. Simply asking your manager a few questions will start the ball rolling:

- What experience have you had of managing flexible working?
- What arrangements were involved?
- Have you worked flexibly yourself?

- Who do you know in this organisation who's working a successful flexible arrangement?

If you hit a dead end consider any internal networks your employer has – such as your women's network or parents' network – and ask the members. Ask HR – they will know of formal applications since these are treated as a permanent change to contract. Ask the people you meet at external networking events – even if it's not going on in your organisation it may be going on elsewhere in your industry.

The idea is to build a personal resource both you and your manager can use to explore flexible working possibilities.

And if you're a woman who's currently working a flexible arrangement, please be open about it. Women often fear negative judgements – particularly in 'hyper masculine' or 'ego driven' cultures. They worry that people will think they're not up to the job and need some sort of extra help. On the contrary: in my experience a senior woman who stands up and says she is working flexibly is likely to be inundated with questions from other women looking for guidance on how to do the same.

A word about moving on or returning to work

According to research funded by the Joseph Rowntree Foundation almost two million workers are stuck in jobs below their skills level; and almost the same number again would like to work if they could do so flexibly.

It can prove more challenging to explore the culture of an organisation when you're an outsider; but doing your research is both possible and worthwhile. Get creative, use your networks and look at what the potential employer is saying publicly. Websites that collect employee feedback – such as Glassdoor – can also be useful. The American site Fairygodboss.com specifically includes ratings for flexible working.

It is also possible to upcycle as you move jobs.

Sally was headhunted for a senior role with a multinational energy company. At that time she was already working a reduced hours arrangement. She knew her prospective employer had a commitment to 'family friendly' working practices but she still needed to persuade them of the possibilities for reduced hours in the role on offer. Sally initially worked three days per week but found the corporate culture was better suited to five short days. Which also fitted in with her caring commitments. Learning to adjust to reduced hours working at senior levels was a challenge for Sally's new employer; but they were willing to work with her to get it right.

At the risk of repeating myself: this is not a book about culture change but about how to upcycle your working arrangement and your work–life balance. Even so, if enough of us upcycle the stories we tell ourselves will also change and so will the culture. Keep that in mind: you're a pioneer embarking on your own little culture change project. One that will benefit you and the people around you. When you've upcycled successfully you can use the same skills to support others.

Applying this to your life

In this chapter we've been looking at how you can identify the flexible working options you might realistically be able to negotiate given your employer's corporate culture, policies and practices. Some questions for you to consider:

- Looking at your employer's corporate culture: who are the current heroes? And what are the heroic stories? Are they people who work long hours and devote all their time to work? Or are they living balanced lives?

- Is the culture uniform or are there functions/departments where it is more open to balanced working? If the latter what can you learn from these more progressive parts of the organisation that will help you structure your own work?

- Based on your knowledge of the corporate culture and of your team are there flexible working arrangements that would work well?

- Are there any that would be inappropriate or hard to maintain?

- Looking at the policies: what flexible working arrangements does your employer currently offer?

- Who do you know internally who's already working flexibly?

- Do you know anyone managing flexible workers?

- What can you learn from them?

- What's your personal business case for flexibility? How can you make it even more persuasive?

- Who else within the organisation might be able to give you guidance on the practicalities of flexible working?

- Is there someone you can enrol as a 'Champion' on your behalf – a senior person who's committed to supporting women/flexible working?

- Where – in your organisation or your industry – have you seen the flexible working arrangement you want happen? Under what circumstances?

- How can you replicate this for yourself?

- Could you start a conversation with your team around how changing working arrangements might benefit your clients/customers?

CHAPTER 6
Possibilities

In this chapter we will consider the flexible working possibilities inherent in your existing role; and I will be sharing techniques you can use to craft that flexibility.

Introduction

Have you ever wondered how your job was created? Who decided what tasks to put together? It's not a question that's likely to turn up at the average pub quiz, but let me tell you anyway.

The art and science of job design has been around since the start of the 20th century and is part of the curriculum for both HR specialists and occupational psychologists. That's not to say they spend much time designing jobs since most organisations already have all the ones they need. Mostly they spend their time tinkering around the edges when a post holder resigns and the job needs to be re-filled. In the past that worked pretty well. The recruiter would simply check whether any of the key tasks had changed; and if so what the likely impact would be on the type of person now needed to fill the job.

All of that's becoming more and more complicated as organisations cope with the frenetic pace of change. Skills are likely to become outdated more quickly; while new ones emerge regularly. The past 20 years have seen massive changes in working practices. Managerial jobs have been changing beyond recognition and emails threaten to engulf our working day. But the biggest challenge appears to be when someone asks '*can this job be worked flexibly?*'

The rapid development of mobile technologies that allow us to be permanently connected to our workplaces regardless of where we are physically has been a key driver of flexible working. On the downside research suggests we are working more hours than ever and experiencing more stress as a result. While employers encourage 'agile working' employees are increasingly left on their own to figure out how to be an 'agile worker' in practice.

In itself, flexible working is not rocket science. But the arrangement we choose will depend on the nature of our job, the sort of flexibility we want – in terms of time and place; and whether we want to reduce our hours. All of which add layers of complexity.

Does that mean we all need to become experts in job design? The short answer is 'no'. But there are tools and techniques you should know about in order to upcycle your job for balance and productivity. That's what we'll be covering in this chapter. Getting clarity – of tasks and outputs – is at the heart of the process. You may be surprised at how much more focussed and productive you become as a result.

Crafting the job you want

The theory

Let's begin with job crafting. Yale professor Amy Wrzesniewski – a key researcher in this area – has discovered that employees routinely make small adjustments to their jobs as a way of improving their engagement and satisfaction.

Job crafting tends to result in more satisfaction at work and greater commitment to your job. It can also increase your attachment to that job and to your employer if it changes the meaning and purpose of work for you. Research shows people job craft all the time – with or without their employer's permission.

Job crafting takes one of three forms:

1. Task crafting involves rearranging or adjusting the activities that make up your job. You may decide to take on more or fewer tasks, expand or diminish their scope or change how you perform them.

2. Relational crafting is where you choose to alter the nature or extent of your interactions with other people.

3. Cognitive crafting means changing how you think about certain parts of your job or reframing how you think about your job as a whole.

It would seem the best results occur when people combine all three.

In their *Harvard Business Review* article 'Turn the job you have into the job you want' Professor Wrzesniewski and her colleagues suggest that successful crafting requires a focus on using more of your strengths and creating value for others. When it comes to relational crafting focus on the people most likely to accommodate you; and work on building trust – particularly with your supervisor or manager.

Since most jobs require us to interact with others few of us have the luxury of job crafting in isolation. Dr Lorenzo Bizzi of California State University has found our job crafting efforts will be influenced by the colleagues with whom we interact regularly on task related issues. These people have expectations of the way we play our roles (check back to Chapter 4) based on the task requirements of their own jobs.

Job crafting is typically about making small adjustments rather than big changes. But where these do impact others you'll need to manage your stakeholders.

In practice

Like many managers my client Christine had a workload that would happily expand to fit all the hours she was willing to devote to it. To make matters worse, she had established a reputation in the business as the person who knew the quickest way to resolve many issues. Consequently she faced a constant battle with emails from people who were happy to delegate their problems to her.

A mother of two, Christine had worked full-time up till now. As her children moved into their teenage years she wanted to carve out more time to spend with them – guiding them through school changes and subject choices. She might even drop down to a four day week if she could see a way of doing it.

We talked about job crafting, and in particular about the pressures placed on her by the expectations of others. She realised she had to manage her interactions with them more effectively.

Starting with the key elements of her job, we identified her priorities and those tasks which took up a lot of her time but did not feed into her objectives. We then looked at how she might begin making changes. Starting with those that were easy to implement we divided them into ones with a small payoff – 'quick wins' – and those with a big payoff – 'bonus opportunities'. A surprising 'bonus opportunity' came with her decision to make herself unavailable to respond to all those niggly little emails outside her key objectives for a fortnight while she concentrated on a big and urgent project.

At the end of the fortnight she reported that most people were simply resolving their own queries and the number of emails she was getting had dropped dramatically. Christine realised she had been allowing the expectations of others to craft her job for her; and resolved to craft her own job in future.

A word of warning here. Most job crafting is unlikely to have a major impact on the design or structure of a job. However, if your employer has any sort of formal job evaluation scheme that feeds into a Reward Policy crafting may have implications for what you earn. While I'd like to tell you the risks are small, I'm not a job evaluation expert. If you're unsure it's wise to run your plans by the Reward experts in your HR department.

Working smarter, not longer

The theory

During my early HR career (many years ago) I worked for one of the GE companies where I was introduced to the Work Out process. Whereas job crafting is typically used to increase meaning and engagement at work; the focus of Work Out is on streamlining work and making it more efficient. It's a systematic approach that I've adapted for my client work.

Work Out is intended as a large scale or 'whole system' process but preparation is typically done on an individual basis. Participants are asked to review and analyse the tasks that make up their jobs. It's a great foundation for upcycling and freeing up time: whether your intention is to work less than full-time or to find space to focus on the more strategic aspects of your work. Here's a summary of my adapted process:

- Start by listing the key tasks required of you in your job. The ones that use the specialist skills and knowledge for which you were hired.
- List any other tasks you regularly do, which take up a lot of your time but don't add to the achievement of your goals. Can you reduce the time spent on these or eliminate them altogether?
- For each task on your list consider whether you can automate it, delegate it or eliminate it.
- Are there any tasks which can be done more efficiently by being done differently?

Even if you currently have nobody to whom you can delegate analysing your job is important – particularly if you're looking to work reduced hours. The smart choice is to eliminate low value tasks and focus on ones that make best possible use of your skills – and add the most value for your employer.

Bearing in mind the influence of others' expectations, map the key network of people with whom you interact and consider the impact on them of making changes. Anticipate reactions and prepare to negotiate.

In their *Harvard Business Review* article 'Make time for the work that matters' Professor Julian Birkinshaw and Jordan Cohen offer a similar approach grounded in their own research. They suggest up to 20% of your working day can be freed up when you eliminate or delegate unimportant 'low value' tasks. According to their findings at least a quarter of a typical knowledge worker's activities are both unimportant to them and their employer and relatively easy to drop, delegate or redesign.

As I was editing this chapter I attended the launch of a new book which looks at how Artificial Intelligence will impact the design of jobs. According to authors Ravin Jesuthasan and John W Boudreau Artificial Intelligence is more likely to eliminate tasks and reinvent jobs than to wipe out a job altogether. Not only is this good news overall, but it's also useful information in the context of our current discussion. In the future we won't need to delegate routine low value tasks to other human beings. We can let the robots take care of them.

So: pick a process, make a plan and commit to making the changes that will upcycle your job.

In practice

In my research and consulting activities I've discovered that for most people work has a way of expanding beyond the time available. We lose control of emails, find ourselves in unnecessary meetings and spend hours on low value activities. Women in particular are renowned for saying 'yes' to requests in the belief that being seen as a supportive colleague will somehow win them brownie points in the promotion game.

The reality – as we saw with Christine earlier – is that the more responsive we are to trivial tasks the more we will encourage them. In Chapter 8 we'll be considering the work of Professor Herminia Ibarra. Here I simply want to mention her recommendation that if we want to progress our careers and develop into leaders we must make time for strategic work. Since it's unlikely our employer will help us reduce our current workload we need to create those opportunities for ourselves. Eliminating trivial and low value work is a way to make the space for that.

Finding flexibility

The theory

Many of us want to find a flexible way of working that enables us to gracefully balance our work with the rest of our lives. For some of us this might be in the form of a reduced hours arrangement – particularly in the early years of parenthood. Alternatively we may want more flexibility in our full-time job. This could be flexibility around location or around the time when we carry out our work. Technology continues to offer us more and more location flexibility; while the global economy can make time flexibility essential.

The four box grid on the next page is one I've developed to help my clients analyse their potential for location and time flexibility – both of which will vary from role to role.

The horizontal axis analyses each job task in turn for time flexibility. The vertical axis looks at location flexibility. For example, box 1 shows a client meeting – an activity which both requires a fixed time and place. In box 2 we have an example of an activity that must be carried out at a specific time but is not limited to a particular location. A monthly report can be produced anywhere assuming access to the necessary technology. Box 3 provides an example of a task which is location dependent but not necessarily time dependent: cash management. To manage cash you must be in the place where the cash is. But you could carry out the task at any time of day or even any day of the week. Finally, in box 4 we have an example of an activity that can be done any time anywhere. Actioning the digital marketing plan simply requires access to a digital device and there may be considerable scope around when the activity is carried out – particularly with the rise of scheduling tools.

The more tasks falling into box 1 the less scope for flexibility. Conversely the more tasks in box 4 the more scope for flexibility. A full box 2 enables you to negotiate location flexibility (i.e. remote working) while a full box 3 supports time flexibility.

If you're about to return to work – or planning to move jobs – using the grid below to analyse a potential job will also show you where the scope lies for negotiation. As we saw in the previous chapter you will – of course – need to do that in the context of the organisation's culture.

Analysing a job for its flexibility potential

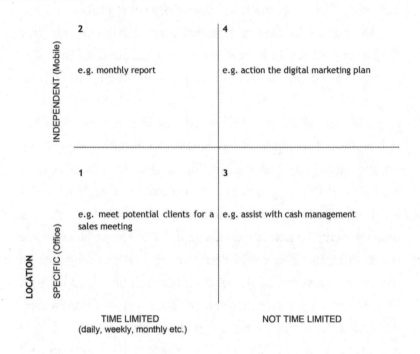

In practice

One of my favourite cartoons shows a female employee negotiating part-time working. When her boss asks if she would be willing to come in on non-working days to complete urgent work she immediately agrees. At which point her colleagues point out all she's achieved is a pay cut.

The cartoon is funny because it's well observed. It seems to me that where many employers are concerned: If you want to work flexibly it's down to you to somehow structure an arrangement that works. I've met many women who tell me they tried working part-time but just ended up exhausted by their efforts to get their job done. A key reason for this is they were effectively trying to squeeze five days' work into three or four.

People rarely stop to consider how effectively they are doing their jobs and – as Robert Pozen from MIT Sloan School of Management has observed – employers continue to evaluate performance based on the number of hours we put in rather than the outputs we produce. If we want to upcycle our flexible working arrangements we need to get smarter about it. Use the tools in this chapter to regularly review how you're doing; and keep your focus firmly on your high value outputs.

Before we leave this chapter a quick word about job-share which is currently undergoing a resurgence in popularity. There's plenty of evidence to demonstrate the advantages of a good job-share arrangement. In my experience when properly set up they work very well. Success depends on thorough forward planning and open, honest conversations between sharers. If you're part of a job-share or considering one you'll find the techniques in this chapter equally appropriate. For example: you might craft the job between you so you each take on the tasks which play to your strengths or provide you with more meaning. Spotting low value tasks that can be eliminated will not only enable you to work more efficiently as a team but also give you more time for that all-important handover.

Whether you choose to job-share or simply to increase the flexibility in your existing role it's likely you'll need to upcycle your skills. We will turn our attention to this in the next chapter.

Applying it to your life

In this chapter we have been looking at the flexible working possibilities inherent in your existing role; and how techniques such as focussing on high value activities and job crafting can enable you to find more flexibility. Some questions for you to consider:

- What sort of flexibility are you looking for: Time? Location? Reduced hours?

- Or are you simply looking to reduce your overall workload and carve out some time for strategic thinking?

- How could you use job crafting to make small adjustments that upcycle your working life?

- What's the likely reaction from stakeholders if you do that?

- How can you influence them?

- What low value activities can you eliminate from your job? What would be the impact on others around you?

- What are the small changes you could make to your working practices that would have the biggest impact on your work–life balance?

CHAPTER 7
Essential skills

In this chapter we will consider the essential skills needed to successfully manage both our work–life balance and our flexible working arrangement.

Introduction

The previous four chapters have focussed on the first two stages of the PROPEL model. In Chapters 3 and 4 we took a deep dive into the meaning of work–life balance and identified our upcycling strategies. Chapters 5 and 6 focussed on the possibilities open to us for upcycling our work.

If we're to succeed we must master some essential skills; and the good news is most of these are not brand new. They're ones you've already been developing as you progress your career. You'll simply need to upgrade some and nuance others.

While the past two decades have seen an explosion in flexible working, there's been a lot less emphasis on training in how to be an effective flexible worker. I suspect that's because many people assume the job is the job regardless of whether you're working a traditional or a flexible arrangement. While that's true to some extent, flexibility does move the goalposts.

A recent US study conducted by the Flex+Strategy Group found that despite the fact most people have some access to flexible working more than half of them had received no training or guidance in how to manage it. It would also seem the number who do receive training has been dropping year on year.

Speaking about the research, CEO and Founder Cali Williams Yost stressed the need for a well-executed corporate strategy around flexibility. In her experience it requires a fundamental re-think in our working practices at all levels. To achieve high performance and wellbeing people need to be trained to be more intentional about their work.

While your employer may not offer specific training around flexible working, it's highly likely they will offer management training that covers many of the skills we will discuss in this chapter. I've grouped the skills you'll need into three categories to help you pinpoint the ones relevant to you: skills for maintaining work–life balance; skills for working reduced hours/job-share; and skills for working flexibly or remotely. In reality there is considerable crossover between categories.

Skills for managing work–life balance

The theory

Despite considerable research into many aspects of work–life balance surprisingly little attention has been given to the skills a person needs to manage it for herself. Dr Almuth McDowall – a leading authority on work–life balance – has however been exploring a competency approach.

By competency we mean the combination of knowledge, skill, behaviour and attitude a person must have or acquire in order to perform effectively. So – for example – it's not enough to understand our boundary management preferences or why we must manage boundaries. We need to develop the behaviours (strategies) that support us to do so. Many of us will be familiar with competencies since employers often use them as a focus for recruitment and development activities.

Dr McDowall has identified eight 'self-management competencies' that help support a good work–life balance. According to her research key skills needed include:

- Time management
- Being able to set and manage priorities
- Managing our boundaries
- Proactively asking for support when needed
- Being able to negotiate and re-negotiate flexible working in practice
- Taking personal responsibility for our work–life balance
- Making adjustments when our work–life balance needs or our circumstances change
- Managing the expectations of others

When it comes to a work–life balance the competency approach is still in its infancy. The list above is a great place to start evaluating your skills and behaviours. You may find some of the competencies resonate more fully with you than do others.

In practice

With the inexorable rise of technologies that keep us permanently connected we often forget we don't need permission from anyone else to switch off. As we've already seen managing boundaries – whether that's the interface between work and non-work or the boundary around how much you're willing to allow work to expand its presence in your life – is absolutely essential. In my workshops it's often the small adjustments people make around boundaries which seem to have the biggest impact.

Skills for working reduced hours/ job-share

The theory

Similarly thin on the ground is research into what skills are needed to successfully work a senior role on reduced hours.

Dr Charlotte Gascoigne has studied the process by which professionals negotiate reduced hours working. She has found that workloads are rarely reduced accordingly. The decision to reduce hours is typically seen as a 'lifestyle choice'; and her research participants did not expect a corresponding reduction in workload when making the change. That said, it's pretty obvious that squeezing five days' work into three or four is a recipe for exhaustion at best and failure at worst. You must take a smarter approach and upcycle your job.

Dr Gascoigne considers the skills of negotiation, boundary management, delegation and forward planning to be essential for success in a reduced hours senior role. She has also found that professionals working reduced hours may be at risk of being judged as unable to meet their employer's needs. This is particularly likely in a corporate culture of 24/7 'Always On' availability. If that's you then job-share may be the more practical alternative.

Employers often find job-share easier to accommodate since – on the face of it – there's no need to restructure tasks or working hours. In my experience however the arrangement comes with its own challenges:

1. You'll need to get on well with your job-share partner. I've heard job-share described as *'a more intense partnership than marriage'*. The arrangement certainly thrives on trust, a common outlook and both partners pulling their weight equally.

2. You'll need to get on well with your manager – and convince them that their own workload will not double when they're managing two rather than one. Writing in the *Harvard Business Review* Amy Gallo points out that managerial support can ensure the success of a job-share regardless of the broader organisational culture.

3. You'll need to manage your stakeholders. That means making sure you and your partner have the infrastructure and processes in place to provide them with a seamless service.

It should come as no surprise that good communication skills are a priority for meeting all three challenges. Communicating well in all directions will create trust – often identified by commentators as the missing ingredient which stalls many flexible working arrangements.

In practice

If you want to work your job on reduced hours then job crafting is your best option for creating a manageable workload according to research by Dr Charlotte Gascoigne and Professor Clare Kelliher.

To work reduced hours successfully you'll also need to upcycle your client management skills. An inability to meet client (or customer) needs is one of the most popular reasons given by managers for refusing a flexible working request. During my research into work–life balance in the legal profession I discovered that in reality clients are rarely the real issue. Most of them are happy to negotiate around your flexible hours unless there's a genuinely tight deadline to meet. Clients – too – will often be working flexibly.

If job-share is your arrangement of choice spending time on preparation with your partner is essential. Over the years I've met a number of successful job-shares and just one that failed. All have confirmed the need for both partners to communicate effectively and trust each other.

Skills for flexible and remote working

The theory

Andy Lake is a flexible working expert whose research has contributed to the development of the BSI's Smart Working Code of Practice. In his book *Smart Flexibility* Andy identifies 20 people skills focussing on self, team and task management which he considers essential for successful flexible and remote working. These include communication, team building and team management skills, negotiation, assertiveness, coaching/mentoring and problem solving. There are no surprises on the list. All the skills can be found in any management training programme. In Andy's view the competencies needed are the same, regardless of work location. What changes is the context. And according to him communication is the skill to prioritise above all others.

At Coventry University Dr Christine Grant is studying the wellbeing of e-workers –people whose work requires the use of technology, often but not always working remotely. She talks about 'digital resilience' which is the skill of managing technology in a way that work and health outcomes are both positive and sustainable.

According to Dr Grant good communication and self-organisation skills, the ability to manage your own work–life balance and being competent at working with Information and Communication Technologies (ICT) are the keys to 'digital resilience'.

While we're on the topic of resilience, many employers are now offering training in this area and yours may be one of them. If not you can take a look at the Robertson Cooper personal resilience model developed by psychologists Professor Ivan Robertson and Professor Sir Cary Cooper. Their free online questionnaire will help you assess how well you manage your resilience based on four components – confidence, social support, adaptability and purposefulness; and to use the results to enhance your skills.

In practice

A few years ago I carried out a survey for a local authority client planning to extend remote working. We asked whether people would prefer to work from home or come into the council's offices. And we were surprised when the majority said they would prefer to continue working in the office. It seems they valued the separation of work and home; along with the social engagement that work gave them.

Remote working is on the rise – but it doesn't suit everybody. One of the biggest disadvantages revealed by my research is the *out of sight, out of mind* syndrome. Remote workers run the risk of being overlooked for promotion and are less likely to be picked for high profile projects. (That's unless you're working as part of a remote team of course.)

Working from home will save you travel time and costs – but make sure you have the skills in place to do it successfully. And if possible try and get into the office from time to time.

Becoming a Balanced Leader

Making the choice to upcycle your job is an act of leadership. You step out of traditional workplace norms. You become a pioneer and role model for others who want to combine work and caring in more creative ways. The next chapter is all about this type of leadership so I've excluded any discussion about leadership skills here.

Applying it to your life

In this chapter we looked at the essential skills needed to successfully manage both our work–life balance and reduced hours, job-share, flexible and remote working arrangements. We concluded by learning that we may also need to upcycle our leadership skills as we pioneer new ways of working. Some questions for you to consider:

- Let's start by identifying the skills you already offer. What makes you valuable to your employer? This might include both technical and people skills along with the internal knowledge you've developed about processes, people and politics that help you get things done.

- How can you leverage the value of these skills and knowledge to help you negotiate the flexible working arrangement you want?

- What skills do you need to upcycle to better manage your work–life balance?

- What skills do you need to upcycle to work reduced hours successfully?

- If you're contemplating a job-share, what skills do you need to upcycle for this?

- What skills do you need to upcycle to work flexibly or remotely?

- Take a look at the list of skills at the end of this chapter. Are there any others that need upcycling?

Once you've read the next chapter you may want to return and consider what skills you need to enhance to grow into a Balanced Leader.

Skills list

Use this list to identify the key skills you need to upcycle and how you will go about doing so (employer training course, book, online resources, etc.).

Assertiveness

Boundaries (setting and managing)

Coaching others

Delegating

Influencing others (navigating organisational politics)

Job crafting

Listening skills

Managing expectations (clients and colleagues)

Mindfulness

Negotiation/generative conversations

Outputs/results focus

Planning

Resilience

Self-management

Storytelling

Technical skills (e.g. ICT for remote working)

Time management

Virtual meetings (running/participating)

Any others that are important for you?

CHAPTER 8
Leadership

In this chapter I introduce the idea of Balanced Leadership as a foundation for your own thinking about the type of leader you want to be.

Introduction

I concluded the previous chapter by asserting that upcycling your job is an act of leadership. If we accept 'guidance' and 'direction' as synonyms for leadership we realise that women have been guiding and directing workplace change for several generations. As I pointed out in Chapter 2 women pressed for changes to working arrangements; and women continue to extend the possibilities for flexibility in their efforts to combine work and family. These are subtle acts of leadership.

It seems we still have a problem seeing women as leaders. Too many of us continue to regard men as more capable of leadership. While the lack of women in senior roles is often explained as down to their lack of ambition, in my experience nothing could be further from the truth. Women do want successful careers. They want to be stretched, challenged and rewarded in exactly the same way as men do. But women don't want to do that at the expense of everything else in their lives. In my experience it's not lack of ambition but a concern about managing work–life balance that causes many women to hold themselves back.

This chapter introduces the concept of Balanced Leadership. It's one I've been thinking about over the past few years; and it's one I believe will resonate with women. My thinking has been influenced by the work of three leading academics: Beverly Alimo-Metcalfe whose research is re-defining the characteristics of leadership; Stewart Friedman whose 'Total Leadership' model embraces the whole of life; and Herminia Ibarra whose research into how we grow into our 'working identity' will guide us on our journey.

The following pages provide a very brief introduction to their work. I hope their ideas encourage you to re-think your own about what it means to be a leader; and to open up new possibilities for your own leadership journey. If their work resonates with you I encourage you to explore further.

A woman and a leader?

Over the past century research into leadership has been dominated by a focus on (predominantly white) men. The original command and control approach of the early 20th century grew increasingly inappropriate in the face of economic uncertainties during the 1970s and 1980s. It was replaced by the idea of the 'heroic' or 'charismatic' leader: a visionary man able single-handedly to lead his organisation out of trouble.

A consequence of the historical focus on male leadership characteristics has been the implicit and enduring widespread assumption that women lack the necessary leadership skills.

Indeed research suggests we're much more likely to attribute leadership success in men to their ability, whereas for women we assume it's down to hard work or sheer luck.

Against this background Beverly Alimo-Metcalfe has been working to create a more inclusive definition of leadership. Professor Alimo-Metcalfe found that men and women define leadership differently. Men tend to see it as bestowing power on subordinates for the good of the organisation. Women on the other hand tend to emphasise relationships and empowerment. Their definition incorporates notions of interdependence, co-operation and connectedness; and of power sharing. All of this is at odds with many of the definitions found elsewhere in the leadership literature.

Having conducted one of the largest and most inclusive studies ever into the nature of leadership Professor Alimo-Metcalf and her colleagues developed a new model of Engaging Leadership. It focusses on serving others and supporting them to display leadership themselves. It encompasses team working, collaboration and connectedness; together with a desire to see the world through the eyes of others and to take on board their concerns, perspectives and ideas.

Engaging Leaders are not seen as 'extraordinary' or 'heroic' but as ordinary, open, humble, accessible and transparent human beings. It's a style of leadership that encourages questioning and challenging the status quo; that creates an environment in which ideas are heard and valued and in which innovation and entrepreneurialism are encouraged. As a consequence a culture that supports development emerges in which the leader becomes a role model for learning; and in which inevitable mistakes become learning opportunities.

Professor Alimo-Metcalfe has pointed out the most conspicuous feature of her model is the 'feminine' perspective on leadership which emphasises partnership, supporting others and encouraging their leadership; and treating leadership as a social process.

Despite widespread adoption of her model – particularly in the public sector – Professor Alimo-Metcalfe has observed that our gendered assumptions about leadership are proving hard to shift. It's no wonder women often experience imposter syndrome when they move into leadership roles.

Total Leadership – aiming for 'four way wins'

Professor Stewart (Stew) Friedman is founder of the Wharton (US) Work/Life Integration Project. Based on many years of research and practice Stew has developed his Total Leadership model: 'Total' because it embraces the whole person and 'Leadership' because it's about creating sustainable change that benefits both the individual and the people around her. The emphasis is on 'four way wins' – for work, family, community and private self.

Professor Friedman has been a long term advocate for work–life balance. Writing in the *Harvard Business Review* as early as 1998 Friedman and colleagues made the case to end what they termed the 'zero-sum' game for work and life. With a shift in workplace demographics they were coming across a growing number of managers – often flying under the radar – approaching work–life challenges differently. These managers were committed to engaging with the 'whole person' at work. Instead of treating work and life as competing priorities they were treating them as complementary: creating the possibility of a win-win outcome for their staff.

Ten years later – again writing in the *Harvard Business Review* – Professor Friedman introduced his 'Total Leadership' process based on the three principles of being real (acting authentically); being whole (acting with integrity) and being innovative (to find creative solutions).

To find more balance in our lives Professor Friedman suggests we design small experiments and try them out for a set period of time. We should aim for a four way win – which means looking for changes that benefit all our life domains. (Think back to our earlier example of Laura in Chapter 3. Setting boundaries enabled her to be present for her family and improved her own wellbeing while resulting in more energy for work.)

When setting goals Friedman recommends we keep in mind the impact on our stakeholders, prioritising the goals they would also like to see happen. Our intention is to pursue small wins that create big change. Massive shifts often fail because they're difficult to manage. According to him the best experiments allow us to try something new while minimising the risks associated with change. Fear of failure is reduced; and as we see results we become inspired to go further – building stakeholder support along the way.

Professor Friedman believes there are more four way wins possible for us than we might imagine – we simply need to know how to look for them; and then find the support and energy to pursue them.

Growing into leadership

Herminia Ibarra has devoted her career to studying how other people navigate career transition; and to identifying how they develop what she calls a 'working identity'. She maintains we rarely arrive in a new job 'fully formed'. More often than not we draw on our existing skills to grow into the person we will become.

It's an idea likely to resonate with those of us who are parents. There's a saying: *'when a child is born so is a mother'* but it's rare for that mother to turn up fully formed, confident and capable. Every small act of parenting she makes will support her growth into her new role.

In her latest book *Act Like a Leader, Think Like a Leader* Professor Ibarra has applied her thinking to the way workplace leaders evolve. Too many organisations – she argues – are taking the wrong approach to leadership development. They start with leadership training then expect people to behave like leaders. In her experience the process actually works the other way round. As we begin making small acts of leadership we feel our way into leadership thinking; and the environment around us reinforces our new identity. In order to think like a leader – therefore – we must begin to act like a leader.

Professor Ibarra suggests that as we step into a bigger leadership role we go through a five stage process. First we become aware of the gap between where we currently are and where we want to be. As a result we begin to add new behaviours to our repertoire but we still hold on to the old ones. At this point it's likely we will backslide and experience obstructions as the people around us encourage our old behaviour. Gradually we begin to 'course correct' as we reflect on our new experiences; and we adjust our goals and behaviours accordingly. Finally, as we internalise our new identity the changes we are making begin to stick.

Within this process we can define for ourselves how we want that bigger leadership role to look. As we explore our emergent leadership identity Professor Ibarra encourages us to be more playful with ourselves. She suggests we explore possible future selves and try on new behaviours lightly to assess which ones suit us and make us feel comfortable. As we proceed we may initially find ourselves feeling inauthentic (experiencing imposter syndrome) but this is all part of working towards becoming the leader we want to be.

Choosing Balanced Leadership

The corporate world needs more women leaders. And those leaders must redefine how they 'do leadership'. Not just for their own benefit but for that of everyone around them. Amidst the constant frenzy of 21st century life we need a way to get more present and be more mindful – so we can make better decisions, head up more balanced organisations and lead more balanced lives. Embracing the notion of Balanced Leadership provides us with an unparalleled opportunity to upcycle the way we live and work.

Balanced Leaders define their own style – just as the female CEOs in a recent study conducted by Associate Professor Andromachi Athanasopoulou did. These women retained typically feminine behaviours such as being more sensitive while supplementing these with more 'masculine' ones. They did this not by fluctuating between 'male' and 'female' behaviours but rather by blending them into what the researchers call a 'gynandrous leadership repertoire' in which they embraced stereotypically masculine behaviours in ways that feel authentic to them.

Balanced Leaders focus on balance in all areas of their lives; and recognise the need to grow into the new way of being they're pioneering.

Are you up for the challenge? Connect with me and let's blaze that trail together.

For the past two years I've been blogging about Balanced Leadership. You'll find lots more food for thought at https://thebalancedleader.wordpress.com/

Applying it to your life

This is not a chapter about developing leadership skills. There are plenty of books and training programmes that offer comprehensive forays into leadership. The purpose of this chapter is to support you in evaluating your ideas about leadership, your own leadership potential and aspirations; and in encouraging you to explore your feelings about embodying these. Some questions for you to consider:

- What have been your assumptions about leadership to date?

- How have you applied these to your life/circumstances?

- Which of the ideas presented in this chapter resonate with you? How might you apply them in your own life?

- Where have you already shown leadership in your life? Is there anything holding you back from acknowledging it as leadership?

- Having read this far into the book how have your ideas about leadership changed?

- How would you choose to define leadership for yourself?

- If you stepped up to Balanced Leadership how would that benefit the people around you (both at work and at home)?

PART 3

POWER TOOLS FOR #UPCYCLING

CHAPTER 9

Introducing positive psychology

Introduction

Whatever we're upcycling, having the right power tools helps. When it comes to upcycling our jobs and our work–life balance the positive psychology kit bag offers some great tools. In this chapter I want to introduce two that I use regularly in my consulting and coaching work: Appreciative Inquiry and Solutions Focus. I'll be giving you a very brief summary of what each is about together with examples of how I've used it in my work.

Positive psychology is the exciting 'new kid on the block' that's been changing the way we think about human potential for the past two decades. Prior to the 21st century much of psychology was focussed on what was wrong with human beings and how to 'fix it'. Then Martin Seligman – speaking to the American Psychological Association (APA) – called for a shift. It was time for psychologists to turn their attention to what was going well and how it might be made even better.

Psychologists such as Barbara Fredrickson – researching the value of positive emotions – had been laying the groundwork for the previous 20 years or so. Mihaly Csikszentmihalyi had begun his search for the optimum conditions to get us into 'flow'; and Dr Seligman himself had shifted his attention from leaned helplessness to a consideration of how we can harness our strengths and values to bring us greater happiness. His speech to the APA led to an exponential growth in 'positive psychology' – with an emphasis on issues such as personal strengths, psychological health and wellbeing, getting into 'flow' and how to create positive teams and institutions. It also earned Seligman the title of father of positive psychology. If you want to learn more about this fascinating subject, Dr Ilona Boniwell's book *Positive Psychology in a Nutshell* is a great introduction.

Appreciative Inquiry

Overview

Based on original work by Professor David Cooperrider (Case Western University) and Suresh Srivastva in the 1980s, Appreciative Inquiry (AI) is a collaborative approach to organisational design and change that is both positive and future focussed. Organisations are seen as living human systems and the stories we tell ourselves within those organisations shape our world. Initially developed as a large group change process AI has been extended to small groups and individual coaching.

Key principles

The organisation is 'alive': human beings in relationship with each other jointly create a living entity that has the potential for both growth and renewal.

The organisation is human. It's made up of the people who create it and it only exists because of these people. It therefore contains all aspects of human life which can, at times be chaotic, emotional, illogical and irrational. Consequently organisations are not neat and tidy; and do not run on orderly lines. This contrasts with earlier 'organisations as machines' perspectives that view people simply as cogs in the process.

The organisation is a system comprising interdependent, inter-reliant and interconnected parts. AI interests itself with the 'pattern' of the system which is made up of patterns of belief, communications, action and reaction, and sense-making. These patterns equate to the 'cultural artefacts' we discussed in Chapter 5.

AI believes in the power of appreciation to promote growth and achieve change. This is in direct contrast to the prevailing belief in the power of criticism to produce change found in many organisations. Our first step when adopting an AI approach is to ask *'what is the behaviour we want to grow?'* rather than *'what is the behaviour we want to stop?'*

When we inquire into an aspect of organisational life our question itself has the power to change things; or at least to begin the change process. This is because questions direct our attention and generate information. The more we ask the more information we collect. For example, when we ask who in our organisation is working flexibly at senior levels we turn our attention to this aspect of organisational life. The more we ask the more examples we're likely to find; and the more potential we have for building on them.

Questions are structured to elicit a positive response. Rather than asking *'can you think of a successful senior level flexible working arrangement in this organisation?'* which might generate the response 'no I can't' we ask *'think of a successful senior level flexible working arrangement you've seen...'* which creates the assumption that the event/state exists making it more likely to generate a positive response.

AI harnesses imagination to create desirable images of the future. These desirable images of how things could be pull people towards them. When people get excited by an imagined future they become motivated to achieve it and organise their behaviour accordingly.

People are motivated differently by their positive and negative emotions. While negative emotions narrow the focus of our attention, they reduce our ability to be creative, manage complexity and take risks. Positive emotions – in the words of Barbara Fredrickson – help us 'broaden and build'. Collaborating with others enables us to find better solutions; while harnessing the positive energy generated becomes a powerful resource for change.

AI adopts a conversation-based perspective. How we talk about the world affects how we see, experience and make sense of the world; and ultimately the way we act in the world. When we change the patterns of conversation we change the world.

AI believes language is an influential tool which can create and generate new meaning between people. One of the ways we use language is to create organisational stories – about *'the way things are done around here'*. When we change these stories we can change behaviour in the organisation; and eventually change the corporate culture.

How I've used it in my work

In Chapter 5 I mentioned that one of my first activities when undertaking a corporate consulting assignment is to survey managers' experience of flexible working and other support for work–life balance. Essentially I'm asking the question: *'where do we already see it happening in this organisation?'* Shining a light on flexible working changes the conversation, identifies resources and opens up new possibilities.

> I used AI to facilitate a discussion about improving work–life balance for a multi-disciplinary team in the NHS. Team members were well aware of the benefits of good work–life balance and wanted to support each other. A variety of working patterns and personal needs had resulted in what seemed to be a complex challenge.
>
> I began by asking team members to vision what good balance would look like for them. We then went on to pinpoint those times when it was already happening and under what circumstances. We were then able to identify the actions needed to make it happen more often.

Solutions Focus

Overview

The roots of Solutions Focus (SF) lie in the brief therapy work of Steve de Shazer and Insoo Kim Berg who developed it as a therapeutic intervention during the 1980s. In contrast with other coaching approaches the focus is on keeping our attention on identifying solutions rather than analysing problems; and on enabling the client to harness her inner wisdom do so.

Key principles

Change is happening all the time. Our aim is to identify and increase useful change. We start by describing our desired end state. How will we know when the problem no longer exists? Asking: 'what else?' uncovers more detail and builds up a rich picture of that desired end state or goal.

There is no 'one right way' of looking at things. Different views may be equally appropriate. Rather than arguing about perspectives, our intention is to agree on what we want to have happen. That is: to create a rich picture of the goal.

Detailed understanding of the 'problem' is generally of little use in our search for the solution. When we get locked into analysing the problem we often get stuck in problem focussed thinking. And as Einstein allegedly said: *'we cannot solve our problems with the same thinking we used when we created them'*.

No 'problem' happens all the time. Finding a solution lies in identifying the circumstances under which the problem is not happening. The idea is to discover what works and do more of it. We do this by asking questions like *'when do you already feel your life is in balance?'* rather than *'when do things go wrong?'*

Small changes in the right direction can be amplified to great effect. Nudging change along in small steps has benefits in time, cost and effort. This type of change follows the path of least resistance.

Scaling is used to pinpoint where we are now in relation to our desired outcome and to measure our progress towards it. Scales are personal and subjective and typically run from zero to ten; with ten being the point at which we've reached our desired outcome. Most people know intuitively where they are on a scale. Progress is made by asking what steps will move them one point along; or asking what they will be doing when they reach the next point.

In their book *The Solutions Focus* Paul Z. Jackson and Mark McKergow refer to SF as a 'big idea about small steps'. No matter how small the individual change, the method harnesses knock on effects to create a bigger impact. When we recognise the systemic nature of organisations we can take small steps that ripple widely across people and departments.

You may already have spotted similarities between the SF approach and AI. The key difference is that SF is typically used in coaching whereas AI lends itself to larger group processes. It is possible to use SF in a group setting – as my example in the next section illustrates.

How I've used it in my work

As part of my research into work–life balance in the legal profession I ran a series of focus groups in participating firms. Traditionally a group of this type would be given a list of items that support work–life balance – such as childcare vouchers, access to flexible working, workshops for mothers and fathers, etc. – and asked to comment on them. There was some concern that approaching things in this way might encourage focus group participants (female lawyers on track to make partner) to ask why their firm didn't offer items on the list. I was also concerned that focussing on lack could generate a negative spiral.

Instead I chose to use a Solutions Focus approach and asked participants to build a picture of what a good work–life balance would look like for them. We then used scaling to rate employers on how well they matched this desirable ideal. While it was purely subjective it provided an insight into how satisfied women were with their employer's existing provisions.

After one of the sessions a woman came up to me saying: *'you didn't mention childcare'* to which my response was *'your group didn't raise childcare as part of their discussion'*. It emerged that the majority of these working mothers – when asked about what would improve their work–life balance – felt childcare was the least of their concerns. Better support from their employer was higher up their agenda.

The Solutions Focus approach believes we are all best placed to solve our own problems. The role of the coach is simply to act as facilitator for the process.

On another occasion I used the Solutions Focus approach with a group of women working in the energy sector. Having asked them to develop a rich picture of what good work–life balance would look and feel like for them one participant said in surprise 'I would have a cleaner'. Single and devoting much of her time to her career, she'd been living with the assumption that having a cleaner would be an indulgence and she ought to be doing her own cleaning. Hiring a cleaner enabled her to make a positive adjustment to her work–life balance by spending non-work time on activities she actually enjoyed.

Again Solutions Focus cuts through what we think we should be doing, or ought to do, and helps identify what we want to do. Then we're more motivated to take steps to make it happen.

Using positive psychology to #Upcycle your life

Allow yourself at least 15 minutes and preferably more to imagine what a balanced life would look like for you.

- Where and when would you be working? Who would you be working with? What would you be doing at home? How would other family members be behaving? What else would tell you that you were living a balanced life? Build a rich picture for yourself with as much detail as possible.

- On a scale of zero to ten – where zero is 'not at all' and ten is 'upcycling done; balance achieved' – where are you now?

- What small steps would get you to the next point on the scale? What will you be doing when you get there?

- What stories are you telling yourself about your possibility for a balanced life?

- What stories does your employer's culture support?

- Could you move the organisational story of 'this is how it is' to a story of possibilities? Who would you need to talk to? What questions would you need to ask?

- Where else could you use the power of questioning to stimulate change?

- When it comes to finding balance, what in your life is already working and how could you do more of it? What would you need to do less of? Who would you need to have a conversation with?

CHAPTER 10
Parting thoughts

If you've read this far rather than just skipping to the final chapter – which only really works for murder mysteries – I hope I've opened your eyes to the tremendous potential you have for upcycling your job and your life. If you've answered the questions in Chapters 3–7 you will have a clearer idea of what that upcycled life could look like.

In the same way that previous generations of women have pressed for progress in the corporate world – rather than waiting for their employer to change – you too can take the power into your own hands.

I've indicated previously that it will make you a pioneer; and a great role model for others. You know that while it's possible it won't necessarily be easy. You'll need to be both brave and vulnerable. (Brené Brown has written some great books on how to manage vulnerability.)

Psychologists talk about our possible future selves; and I want to encourage you to grow into your best possible self: to play your biggest game, live your biggest life and make your biggest contributions.

All too often we're told women lack ambition, skills or confidence in themselves. I don't believe any of that. You're a working parent *and* an ambitious professional. You've come this far and I know you can go further. What's been lacking so far is a way to find real balance in your life.

The upcycling ideas you've found in this book will help you tailor a future that fits you, your family and your employer. They show you a way to change the conversation. The corporate world badly needs women like you to step up and redefine leadership in more balanced ways.

Are you ready to make the shift? Ready to be part of a new generation of Balanced Leaders?

Connect with me:

- Join one of my Balanced Leader group programmes or one day Crafting Quality Flexible Jobs masterclasses.
- Sign up for Balanced Leader Bespoke coaching.
- Learn more about me and my services on my website: www.sustainableworking.co.uk
- You'll also find links to the Job Upcycling Community and Information Exchange group; my Balanced Leader blog and my newsletter sign up on the website.
- Follow @GrownUpBalance on Twitter (and take a look at the lists I've been curating to help you #Upcycle Your Job).

Together let's finish the corporate revolution our grandmothers started.

Anna Meller

London, December 2018

Acknowledgements

Grateful thanks to Barbara and Robert Green without whose love and support this book would not have been published.

Thanks to Jonathan Swan for feedback on the early draft and to my beta readers: Rebekah Bostan, Mandy Garner, Katie Hodgson, Harriet Lavender and Jane Middleton whose comments resulted in a superior final version.

Thanks also to Rachel Bridgman and Inge Woudstra Van Grondelle for their comments on the early draft of Chapter 1.

And thanks to Alison Jones and her team at Practical Inspiration Publishing for turning a vague idea into the reality you've just read.

References

Chapter 1

Boston Consulting Group *Dispelling the Myths of the Gender 'Ambition Gap'* April 2017. Available from www.bcg.com/en-gb/publications/2017/people-organization-leadership-change-dispelling-the-myths-of-the-gender-ambition-gap.aspx [accessed 3 January 2019]

Boston Consulting Group Report *Getting the Most from Your Diversity Dollars* June 2017. Available from http://image-src.bcg.com/Images/BCG-Getting-the-Most-from-Your-Diversity-Dollars-June-2017_2_tcm38-161866.pdf [accessed 3 January 2019]

Boushey H *Finding Time: The Economics of Work–Life Conflict* (Harvard University Press 2016)

Catalyst Knowledge Center *Women on Corporate Boards Globally*. Available from www.catalyst.org/knowledge/women-corporate-boards-globally [accessed 3 January 2019]

Chartered Management Institute News 'The search for the missing middle: CMI women launches in hunt for true gender diversity' November 2016. Available from www.managers.org.uk/insights/news/2016/november/the-search-for-the-missing-middle-cmi-women-launches-in-hunt-for-true-gender-diversity [accessed 3 January 2019]

EUROFOUND Report EF0699 *First European Quality of Life Survey: Time Use and Work–Life Options Over the Life Course* 2007. Available from www.eurofound.europa.eu/publications/report/2007/quality-of-life/first-european-quality-of-life-survey-time-use-and-work–life-options-over-the-life-course [accessed 3 January 2019]

Hannon K 'Inspired or frustrated women go to work for themselves' *The New York Times* 3 October 2017. Available from www.nytimes.com/2017/10/03/business/women-entrepreneur-career.html [accessed 3 January 2019]

Hobson B (ed) *Worklife Balance: The Agency & Capabilities Gap* (Oxford University Press 2014)

HR News 'Working mothers hit by lost earnings due to inflexible business cultures'. Available from http://hrnews.co.uk/working-mothers-hit-1-3-trillion-lost-earnings-due-inflexible-business-culture-2 [accessed 3 January 2019]

Institute for Fiscal Studies Briefing Note BN223 *Wage Progression and the Gender Wage Gap: The Causal Impact of Hours of Work* 2018

Joseph Rowntree Foundation Report *How Flexible Hiring Could Improve Business Performance and Living Standards* January 2016

Mainiero L A & Sullivan S E 'Kaleidoscope careers: An alternative explanation for the "opt out" revolution' *Academy of Management Executive*, 19 (1) (2005)

Patty A 'Being a "mumpreneur" is an option of last resort for most mums', *The Sydney Morning Herald* 5 May 2016. Available from www.smh.com.au/business/workplace/being-a-mumpreneur-is-an-option-of-last-resort-for-most-mums-20160504-golplr.html [accessed 3 January 2019]

Peacock L 'Maria Miller: Workplace designed "by men for men"' *The Telegraph* 10 April 2013. Available from www.telegraph.co.uk/women/womens-business/9984107/Maria-Miller-Workplace-designed-by-men-for-men.html [accessed 3 January 2019]

Pregnant Then Screwed website. Available from http://pregnantthenscrewed.com [accessed 3 January 2019]

Reid E 'Why some men pretend to work 80-hour weeks' *Harvard Business Review* April 2015. Available from https://hbr.org/2015/04/why-some-men-pretend-to-work-80-hour-weeks [accessed 3 January 2019]

Sabelis I & Schilling E 'Editorial: Frayed careers: Exploring rhythms of working lives' *Gender Work and Organisation*, 20 (2) (March 2013)

Sandberg S *Lean In: Women, Work and the Will to Lead* (W H Allen 2013)

Telegraph reporters 'Thousands of working women forced into low paid, low skilled jobs after returning from career breaks' *The Telegraph* 14 November 2016. Available from www.telegraph.co.uk/women/life/thousands-of-working-women-forced-into-low-paid-low-skilled-jobs [accessed 3 January 2019]

Williams J C (ed) *The Flexibility Stigma* (Wiley-Blackwell 2013)

Women's Business Council *Maximising Women's Contribution to Future Economic Growth* June 2013

Working Families *Modern Families Index 2018*. Available from www.workingfamilies.org.uk/wp-contentuploads/2018/01/UK_MFI_2018_Long_Report_A4_UK.pdf [accessed 3 January 2019]

Chapter 2

Galinsky E & Johnson A A *Reframing the Business Case for Work–Life Initiatives* (Families and Work Institute 1998)

Higgins J M & McAllaster C 'If you want strategic change, don't forget your cultural artefacts' *Journal of Change Management*, 4 (1) (March 2004)

Kalliath T & Brough P 'Work–life balance: A review of the meaning of the construct' *Journal of Management & Organization*, 14 (3) (July 2008)

Kelliher C & Anderson D 'Doing more with less? Flexible working practices and the intensification of work' *Human Relations*, 63 (1) (January 2010)

Kossek E E, Lewis S & Hammer L B 'Work–life initiatives and organizational change: Overcoming mixed messages to move from the margin to the mainstream' *Human Relations*, 63 (1) (January 2010)

McDowall A & Kinman G 'The new nowhere land? A research and practice agenda for the "always on" culture' *Journal of Organizational Effectiveness: People and Performance*, 4 (3) (2017)

Working Families *Hours to Suit: Working Flexibly at Senior and Managerial Levels* Volumes 1 & 2 2007. Available from www.workingfamilies.org.uk/research-publications/page/5 [accessed 3 January 2019]

Chapter 3

Ampofo L *Podcast #84: Tech & Work Life Balance with Anna Cox* Digital Mindfulness. Available from https://digitalmindfulness.net/84-tech-work–life-balance-anna-cox [accessed 3 January 2019]

Crossfield S, Kinman G & Jones F 'Crossover of occupational stress in dual career couples' *Community Work & Family*, 8 (2) (2005)

Digital Boundaries 'What are microboundaries?' Available from https://digitalboundariesresearch.wordpress.com/home/what-are-microboundaries [accessed 3 January 2019]

Huffington A 'How to succeed? Get more sleep' TED Women 2010. Available from www.ted.com/talks/arianna_huffington_how_to_succeed_get_more_sleep?language=en [accessed 3 January 2019]

Jones F & Fletcher B 'An empirical study of occupational stress transmission in working couples' *Human Relations*, 46 (7) (July 1993)

Kinman G 'How to "switch off" from a stressful day' *OP Matters*, 36 (November 2017) a BPS DOP publication

Kossek E E & Lautsch B A *CEO of Me: Creating a Life That Works in the Flexible Job Age* (Prentice Hall 2007)

Ofcom *Fast Facts*. Available from www.ofcom.org.uk/__data/assets/pdf_file/0023/105926/Fast-facts.PDF [accessed 3 January 2019]

Revell T 'One day without notifications changes behaviour for two years' *New Scientist* 3 August 2017. Available from www.newscientist.com/article/2142807-one-day-without-notifications-changes-behaviour-for-two-years [accessed 3 January 2019]

Wall M 'Smartphone stress: Are you a victim of "always on" culture?' *BBC News* 14 August 2014. Available from www.bbc.co.uk/news/business-28686235 [accessed 3 January 2019]

Chapter 4

Lupu I 'Your feelings about work–life balance are shaped by what you saw your parents do' *Harvard Business Review* 30 October 2017. Available from https://hbr.org/2017/10/your-feelings-about-work–life-balance-are-shaped-by-what-you-saw-your-parents-do [accessed 3 January 2019]

Super D E 'A life-span, life-space approach to career development' *Journal of Vocational Behaviour*, 16 (3) (June 1980)

Chapter 5

Ressler C & Thompson J *Why Work Sucks and How to Fix It: The Results-Only Revolution* (Penguin Group 2008)

Rutherford S *Women's Work, Men's Cultures: Overcoming Resistance and Changing Organizational Cultures* (Palgrave Macmillan 2011)

Stewart E & Bivand P *Report: How Flexible Hiring Could Improve Business Performance and Living Standards* Joseph Rowntree Foundation January 2016. Available from www.jrf. org.uk/report/how-flexible-hiring-could-improve-business-performance-and-living-standards [accessed 3 January 2019]

Chapter 6

Birkinshaw J & Cohen J 'Make time for the work that matters' *Harvard Business Review* September 2013

Bizzi L 'Network characteristics: When an individual's job crafting depends on the jobs of others' *Human Relations*, 70 (4) (April 2017)

Jesuthasan R & Boudreau J W *Reinventing Jobs: A 4-step Approach for Applying Automation to Work* (HBR Press 2018)

Pozen R C 'Stop working all those hours' *Harvard Business Review* June 2012

Ulrich D, Kerr S & Ashkenas R *The GE Work-Out: How to Implement GE's Revolutionary Method for Busting Bureaucracy & Attacking Organizational Problems – Fast* (McGraw Hill 2002)

Wrzesniewski A, Berg J M & Dutton J E 'Turn the job you have into the job you want' *Harvard Business Review* June 2010

Chapter 7

BSI Smart Working Code of Practice press release. Available from www.bsigroup.com/en-GB/about-bsi/media-centre/press-releases/2016/january/New-Smart-Working-Code-of-Practice-announced [accessed 3 January 2019]

Coventry University ework–life balance webpage. Available from https://ework.coventry.ac.uk [accessed 3 January 2019]

Gallo A 'How to make a job sharing situation work' *Harvard Business Review* September 2013

Gascoigne C PhD Thesis: *Part-Time Working Arrangements for Managers and Professionals: A Process Approach*. Available from https://core.ac.uk/download/pdf/29409832.pdf [accessed 3 January 2019]

Gascoigne C & Kelliher C 'The transition to part-time: How professionals negotiate "reduced time and workload" i-deals and craft their jobs' *Human Relations*, 71 (1) (January 2018)

Kratz G 'Survey shows flex benefits boosted by training' *Flexjobs Employer Blog* 2 May 2018. Available from www.flexjobs.com/employer-blog/survey-shows-flex-benefits-boosted-by-training [accessed 3 January 2019]

Lake A *Smart Flexibility: Moving Smart and Flexible Working from Theory to Practice* (Gower Publishing 2013)

McDowall A & Lindsay A 'Work–life balance in the police: The development of a work–life balance self-management competency framework' *Journal of Business and Psychology*, 29 (3) (January 2014)

Robertson Cooper personal resilience model. Available from www.robertsoncooper.com/iresilience [accessed 3 January 2019]

Chapter 8

Alimo-Metcalfe B 'Developments in gender and leadership: Introducing a new "inclusive" model' *Gender in Management*, 25 (8) (2010)

Athanasopoulou A, Moss-Cowan A, Smets M & Morris T 'Claiming the corner office: Female CEO careers and implications for leadership development' *Human Resource Management*, 57 (2) (March–April 2018)

Friedman S D 'Be a better leader, have a richer life' *Harvard Business Review* April 2008

Friedman S D, Christensen P & DeGroot J 'Work and life: The end of the zero sum game' *Harvard Business Review* Nov–Dec 1998

Ibarra H, *Act Like a Leader, Think Like a Leader* (HBR Press 2015)

Chapter 9

Boniwell I *Positive Psychology in a Nutshell* (Personal Well-Being Centre 2006)

Fredrickson B L 'What good are positive emotions?' *Review of General Psychology*, 2 (3) (September 1998)

Jackson P Z and McKergow M *The Solutions Focus: The SIMPLE Way to Positive Change* (Nicholas Brealey Publishing 2002)

Lewis S *Positive Psychology and Change* (John Wiley & Sons Ltd 2016)

Lewis S, Passmore J & Cantore S *Appreciative Inquiry for Change Management: Using AI to Facilitate Organizational Development* (Kogan Page Ltd 2008)

About the author

For the past 25 years Anna Meller has specialised in work–life balance issues and their impact on women's careers. Her consultancy work has supported a range of employers in the private, public and not for profit sectors to improve work–life balance provision for their staff. She has considerable experience of coaching senior managers to improve their work–life balance – adopting a pragmatic and evidence based approach. She continues to share her expertise with a wide range of audiences both as a speaker and regular blogger.

Anna works with ambitious professional women seeking to combine a satisfying corporate career with a balanced family life. Her focus is on empowering them towards better choices so they can make their fullest contribution at work and live a life in balance. To guide her coaching and training services Anna has developed an innovative model (PROPEL) which draws on positive psychology, her own published research and her consulting experience.

Anna has researched and written three ground breaking reports into work–life balance challenges in Professional and Financial Services and her previous book on how to get the best from part-time workers was published by the Chartered Institute of Personnel and Development. She has worked as an accredited consultant to the government's Work–Life Balance Challenge Fund and since 2009 she has been an active member of the BPS Division of Occupational Psychology's working group on Work–Life Balance.

Anna served as a trustee for the charities New Ways to Work and PARENTS AT WORK which subsequently merged to form the UK charity Working Families. Prior to starting on her work–life balance journey she had a successful early career in HR – mostly in the Financial Services sector. She has a Master's Degree in Organisational Behaviour and is a Chartered Fellow of the Chartered Institute of Personnel and Development.

Learn more about Anna on her website: www.sustainableworking.co.uk

Index